ON THE EDGE OF SURVIVAL

Also by Spike Walker

Alaska: Tales of Adventure from the Last Frontier (editor)

Coming Back Alive: The True Story
of the Most Harrowing Search and Rescue Mission
Ever Attempted on Alaska's High Seas

Nights of Ice: True Stories of Disaster
and Survival on Alaska's High Seas

Working on the Edge: Surviving in the World's Most
Dangerous Profession: King Crab Fishing on
Alaska's High Seas

ON THE EDGE
OF SURVIVAL

A Shipwreck, a Raging Storm,
and the Harrowing Alaskan Rescue
That Became a Legend

SPIKE WALKER

St. Martin's Press ≉ New York

www.stmartinspress.com

ISBN 978-0-312-28634-7

First Edition: October 2010

10 9 8 7 6 5 4 3 2 1

To Peter and Christina MacDougall,
as the Northern Lights danced over Sitka

ON THE EDGE OF SURVIVAL

ONE

Slammed right and left by battering, 60 mph wind gusts, blinded by snow squalls at the leading edge of an Arctic storm, search and rescue pilot Lieutenant David Neel was doing his best, early on that cold December morning in 2004, to shake off the sudden bouts of vertigo and keep his H-60 helicopter on course and in the air. Flying along over the gray and white, foam-streaked waters of the Bering Sea, Neel maintained an altitude of just three hundred feet, and no more, to prevent icing as the tall, clutching storm waves lumbered past below. He and his crew had been ordered to Dutch Harbor, where they would refuel and prepare to launch out on an emerging crisis: The *Selendang Ayu*, a giant of a freighter, a 738-foot-long cargo ship bound for China with over 60,000 metric tons of Pacific Northwest soybeans, had apparently lost her engine while following the Great Circle route across those same, intractable waters 170 miles northwest of Dutch Harbor. With some 455,000 gallons of bulk oil stored in her tanks, and twenty-six sailors trapped aboard her, the freighter was now drifting on a collision course with the hull-crushing shores of the Aleutian Islands.

If no one was able to alter her freewheeling advance, and efforts either to restart her engine or pass a towline to her failed, the freighter would soon be driven onto the rocks of Unalaska Island inside the largest maritime seabird nesting area in all of North America. Should an oil spill ensue—a distinct possibility, given the furious, wind-driven seas now propelling the ship along—the impact on those vulnerable creatures could be disastrous, the damage to the environment largely irreparable.

The Panamax-class vessel, the largest of the bulk freighters whose hull could still fit through the Panama Canal, was said to be drifting beam-to the pummeling waves. Some of the prodigious breakers slamming into her and driving her toward shore were reportedly as large as freight train boxcars. At times, the wayward vessel was rolling so wildly from side to side, that the six hundred or so feet of her massive deck was tilting almost vertically.

The weather reports, too, were equally alarming. A storm packing blizzard snows with peak wind gusts approaching hurricane force was currently drafting down out of Russia's Siberian Arctic. Accelerating as it came, the cold front had marched down over the polar ice pack, and was now racing unhindered across the vast, open reaches of the Bering Sea.

Dave Neel was certain, however, that well before the peak of the storm reached them, he and his crew would be sent to the scene with orders to hoist as many of the sailors as possible off the *Selendang Ayu*'s deck before she sank, ran aground, or rolled over. But he also knew that plucking survivors off the heaving deck of a freighter careening through high seas wouldn't be easy; and that doing so in as little time as possible would be absolutely imperative.

Born and raised in Vian, Oklahoma—a town of just 1,200 people, surrounded by farmland—Dave Neel grew up hunting and fishing, was a fifth-generation Oklahoman, and the son of a bricklayer. His people worked in the construction trade. Dirt moving. Concrete pouring. Home building. His parents raised him and his brothers in a traditional, God-fearing, Baptist belief system, one centered around hard work, honest living, and fair play.

Neel knew the H-60 Jayhawk helicopter well. He'd flown them for years in the army, and also on a tour for the Coast Guard (CG) out of Clearwater, Florida. But the base outside Kodiak was this aviator's ultimate destination, a place reserved for the Coast Guard's most trusted and experienced pilots. Only second-tour aviators or better were sent there. In fact, famed Alaskan chopper pilot Russ Zullick was one of Dave Neel's best friends.

Just twelve hours before, Neel and his crew had been sitting in the cargo hold of a C-130, crossing the Shumagin Islands, when Commander (Cdr.) Bill Deal called him forward into the aircraft's cockpit and told him of the crisis building in the Bering Sea. Their C-130 was being diverted to Cold Bay. An H-60 would be waiting. Neel and his crew needed to start planning the rescue.

Recognizing a true crisis in the making, Coast Guard officials had also ordered the cutter *Alex Haley*, to the scene. In addition, they'd dispatched several tugboats, including the oceangoing tug *Sidney Foss* and the harbor tug *James Dunlap* to try to intercept the drifting giant before it ran aground, scattering fuel, cargo, and bodies along the wild, inhospitable shores of Unalaska Island.

Cdr. Matt Bell, the captain on the Coast Guard cutter *Alex Haley*, was about 150 miles away, monitoring the actions of a fleet of codfish longliners, when he received word of the errant freighter's path and location. Bell and his crew were just winding down from fifty or so days of patroling the westernmost reaches of the Bering Sea along the U.S./Russia border, and were about to stand down and steam back to Kodiak for a well-deserved bit of R & R. But now Bell was ordered to locate the vessel, and to assess the situation.

Riding a quartering sea, and moving in the direction of the freighter with all possible urgency, Cdr. Bell set out in hot pursuit of the freighter. However, because the seas were rough, the *Alex Haley* could only move at ten knots (11 mph), and it would be a number of hours before they would catch up with the *Selendang Ayu*. But with half a dozen engineers reportedly among the vessel's crew, Cdr. Bell thought the *Ayu*'s crew might get their engine back up and running before he even caught sight of her.

Standing six feet tall, and weighing a lean 170 pounds, Cdr. Bell was well suited for the duty at hand. Raised in Georgia by family-oriented parents, he was taught the fundamentals of discipline, work, and academic achievement, a lifestyle that was also accompanied by robust outdoor living.

As a small boy, his first exposure to the sea was while camping and fishing for Spanish mackerel at the water's edge of Wrightsville Beach, North Carolina. During those impressionable years, the Coast Guard bug bit him hard, for he often observed the gleaming white patrol boats cruising the inlets and passageways that wind their way through the beautiful archipelago of islands that make up that seaboard region.

"Our summer house was on the inland waterways there," he recalls. "You had to take the pass down through all the back bays to get to the jetty before you could get out to the ocean."

Bell's father, a Marine formerly stationed on Okinawa, was a "hunter-camper-fisher," says Bell. "I think he was handed a fishing pole to hold before he could even walk." Along with four brothers and one sister, Matt Bell took naturally to the outdoors. Never bothered by seasickness, he loved fishing with his father, and joined him every chance he got.

"I don't know if I could even name a more patriotic guy than my father," he says. "Pledge of Allegiance. Love of God and country. My dad believed that serving one's country was both a duty and an honor."

In 1985, Matt Bell joined the Coast Guard. In a very real sense, it seems Cdr. Bell had been headed into the military from the get-go. Surviving boot camp, he was quickly scooped up and sent to Officer Candidate School (OCS). Steady promotions followed solid tours of duty out of the port cities of New Orleans and San Francisco. One of Cdr. Bell's first SAR (search and rescue) cases was picking up debris off the Florida coast after the space shuttle *Challenger* exploded, and its entire crew was killed.

In 1987, Cdr. Bell and his family were assigned to the base in Kodiak, Alaska. At that time he began serving on board Coast Guard cutter patrols in the Bering Sea.

Now, some seventeen years later, and a veteran at navigating those untamed waters, Cdr. Bell pointed the *Alex Haley* in the direction of the disabled freighter, and gave chase.

Eventually, as the *Alex Haley* began to close in on the drifting hulk, Cdr. Bell's officer of the deck (OD) was able to make radio contact with the skipper of the *Selendang Ayu*. It was still dark out when they finally caught up with her. Cdr. Bell and his executive officer (X/O), Lieutenant Commander (LCDR) Phil Thorne, stepped out on the flying bridge for a better look.

"Wow! She's a big one!" said Bell, peering at the long, well-lighted wheelhouse and wave-thrashed deck through his powerful field glasses. "We're sure going to need those tugs."

Inside the C-130 being diverted to Cold Bay, Dave Neel returned to the cargo area, grabbed his maps, and gave fellow co-pilot Lt. Doug Watson the "quick skinny" on the situation. Next, he presented the news to flight mechanic Petty Officer 2nd Class Brian Lickfield, and rescue swimmer Petty Officer 3rd Class Aaron Bean. Then, he sat and did some brainstorming: "How much gas would it take to reach the scene? How long will I be able to remain there?

How many people can I carry in the H-60 in a single load?"

Initially, Neel calculated that he could carry nine of the stranded sailors per load. Flying the H-60 helicopter directly to the scene—its call sign CG6020—they'd gather them up and take them immediately to Dutch Harbor, top off the fuel tanks again, and rush back for more of the *Selendang Ayu*'s crew. He and his flight crew would make the turnaround in Dutch Harbor in record time.

Meanwhile, Cdr. Doug Cameron, the officer in charge of CG6021, the other H-60 Jayhawk, would hoist the second load of nine off the freighter. That would be eighteen saved, leaving just eight, including the ship's captain, to go. Neel and Watson would race back then, hover in close and, if all went well, load up the last of the survivors in as little as fifteen minutes, and they'd be out of there.

But if things should go sideways on them, there were certain realities to consider. For one, the edge of the polar ice pack was now floating just north of the Pribilof Islands, which meant that the waters of the Bering Sea, at that time of the year, would be only a couple of degrees above freezing. In addition, their mission would draw them out over those wind-ravaged waters at about the same time the heart of the storm reached them.

The moment their C-130 touched down in Cold Bay, Dave Neel called Kodiak and spoke with Cdr. Bob Phillips, his ops officer. He wanted to get a better picture of what, exactly, was happening. Phillips told him to stand down on launching the H-60 and await further instructions.

"Hold tight there in Cold Bay," said Phillips. "We're sending another H-60 down. It'll be there later tonight. So far, it looks like you guys might not have to go out, because the oceangoing tugboat *Sidney Foss* is responding. So just stand fast for now."

It was well after dark when the second H-60 arrived from its base on Kodiak Island. Pilots Guy "Yogi" Pierce and Larry Quedado (since deceased) had flown over with it. But with no room left inside the hangar, they were forced to park it outside on the snow-covered runway.

Born and raised in Cranford, New Jersey, fellow pilot Doug Watson was five foot ten, weighed 180 pounds, had sandy blond hair, and was widely recognized as a superb helicopter pilot. He had earned a bachelor's degree in aeronautical science from Embry-Riddle Aeronautical University in Daytona Beach, Florida. Trained, initially, to be a professional or corporate pilot, Watson was also a certified flight instructor.

Signing on with the Coast Guard was an unusual move for someone with his background. He'd attended Officer Candidate School for eighteen months in Pensacola, Florida, then spent another six weeks in Mobile, Alabama, learning to fly the legendary H-60 Jayhawk helicopter. For the next four years he flew missions out of Air Station Clearwater on the Florida coast, before joining the exceptional band of flyboys at Air Station Kodiak.

As a seasoned pilot, now several years into his Alaskan tour, Doug Watson had, of course, been in some very tight spots of his own. Should they need him to fly on such an icy, windswept night, he felt fully up to the challenge.

While outside an arctic wind raked the frozen ground, inside Bill and Mary Cochran's hospitable Cold Bay Lodge, Dave Neel, Doug Watson, Aaron Bean, and Brian Lickfield—and their Coast Guard brothers—sat themselves down to a hearty Alaskan meal of steak and king crab, with all the trimmings.

After dinner, Dave Neel and Doug Watson had withdrawn to their respective rooms and were fast asleep when word of the developing drama reached them. It was flight mechanic Joe Metzler who delivered the news: They were to launch their H-60 as soon as possible.

Outside, it was pitch dark. Numbing winds driving a blizzard snow were howling across the runway and throughout the Aleutian Islands, creating an aviator's nightmare over much of the Bering Sea. The tugboat *Sidney Foss*'s efforts to take the huge ship in tow had ultimately failed. Metzler informed them that they were to preposition themselves in Dutch Harbor, where they would stand by and await further orders.

Long on experience in Alaskan search and rescue missions, thirty-eight-year-old flight mechanic (hoist operator, or winchman, in laymen's terms) Brian Lickfield felt uneasy about the situation. After partaking of that hearty Alaskan dinner, he went to bed sporting a knot in the pit of his stomach, one that refused to go away. It proved to be a restless night for Lickfield. A worrisome voice in his head kept telling him, "It's not over yet. It's not near over. They may still need us out there."

With fourteen years of experience hoisting survivors off boats, and plucking the lost and imperiled out of various predicaments, Lickfield had Alaska in his bones and was aware of the primitive unpredictability of the place. So he was not overly surprised when, late that same night, he received word that everything had "gone to hell" during the salvage operation under way in the Bering Sea. It was Dave Neel who shook him awake.

"Suit up, Brian," he said. "We're going."

Raised in a sports-oriented family in Silverthorne, Colorado, located in the mountains outside of Denver, rescue swimmer Aaron Bean had aspirations, as a little boy, of

one day becoming an Olympic competitor. He began swimming laps in a pool when he was just an adolescent, eventually covering as much as three miles of water in a single
practice at the ten-thousand-foot-high training facilites in
the ski resort village of Breckenridge.

Always in superb physical condition, Aaron was not
quite twenty-one years old when, having completed the
Coast Guard's boot camp in Cape May, New Jersey, and
another year as a physical fitness instructor there, he entered the five-month airman training program at Atlantic
City. The instructors put him and his fellow aspiring rescue swimmers through such physical and emotional extremes that nearly half of his classmates eventually quit,
or were eliminated.

But "Bean," as his friends often call him, was better
prepared than most, and could perform as many as 2,500
push-ups in a single workout. He was just twenty-two
when, in the spring of 2004, he arrived in Kodiak, and
began his tour of duty there as a fully trained and certified rescue swimmer. Now, on this cold, blustery Alaskan
night, Aaron Bean was about to embark on a rescue mission
to the Bering Sea, the intensity of which would forever
mark his life.

By eight P.M. on the same evening that he and his crewmates arrived in Cold Bay, they took possession of the fully
fueled H-60 Jayhawk helicopter waiting for them. Word
had it that somehow, in the fifty-knot (57 mph) winds and

twenty-five-foot seas, the crew of the tugboat *Sidney Foss* had managed to get a hauser line on the giant freighter and take her in tow. "We're not going anywhere tonight," Bean was informed. "Unless their towline breaks. And if that happens, this could become the mother of all SAR cases."

After inhaling the sumptuous meal, Bean had retired to the soft comfort of his bunk when, in the black of night, a hand shook him awake. It was Dave Neel, his flight commander.

"Bean, get your gear," he said matter-of-factly. "The towline has parted."

Now in the cockpit of his H-60, closing steadily on Dutch Harbor, Lt. Dave Neel continued to apply a fundamental part of his philosophy about flying in Alaska. "Whenever you can, get out over open water and travel where the ground can no longer hurt you."

Although he could see, most of the time, that they were flying over open water, the atmospheric conditions, as the cold, gray dawn emerged, were so intense that each time they flew into one of the snow squalls, their superso-phisticated Doppler weather radar proved to be of little use. The precipitation inside the icy weather cells was so concentrated that it kept painting false returns on his radar screen, and delivering unsettling readings that moun-tainous terrain lay just ahead. This kept the chief navigator,

Doug Watson, busy making repeated time and course checks on his map, and pulling up GPS (Global Positioning System) data to fix upon their ever-changing positions along the way.

Crabbing sideways then, with the nose of their H-60 pointing into the wind and their radar screen cocked to one side, they would disappear into each new island of blizzard snow, bouncing up and down as they moved in sharp, erratic jerks.

Flying along on the Bering Sea–side of the Alaska penninsula, Neel and his crew of helo CG6020 got their tails kicked the entire way by air turbulence. Cutting across the surf breaking over the sandbars at the entrance to False Pass, they passed the active, smoking, red-rimmed peak of Mt. Shishaldin on Unimak Island. At the far end of the island, they powered by the lighthouse at Cape Sarichef. The old facility had been completely destroyed in 1946 when a 120-foot-high tsunami swept it away, killing all six Coast Guardsmen stationed there at the time.

Neel and Watson then crossed the infamous, crab boat–eating waters of Unimak Pass. Reaching the nearest edge of Unalaska Island, they began circling around the backside of the eighty-five-mile-long, volcano-studded island. Slammed right and left by williwaws—invisible fists of mountain-born wind—Dave Neel continued on to Dutch Harbor. As he drew nearer to that famous fishing port, he was forced to shoot a low visibility approach. "It was a terrible morning," he recalls. "The wind never stopped."

Neel guided the H-60 to a landing on a desolate corner of the icy, wind-raked runway just ninety minutes after departing from Cold Bay. Once on the ground, he and his crew rushed to fill the aircraft's fuel tanks, and to make sure that everything was shipshape and ready to go at a moment's notice.

Lt. Doug Cameron and his crew were about an hour behind Neel's chopper. While flying there during the early morning, it became so dark inside several of the snow squalls that Cameron was forced to turn on his instrument panel lights, something that "doesn't happen very often," he recalls. "It was already approaching fifty knots in the Bering Sea. It was a really nasty day."

Glad to be safely on the ground in Dutch Harbor, Doug Cameron shut down the H-60's engine and climbed out onto the ice-covered runway to stretch his legs. Immediately, an invisible wall of wind funneling around nearby Ballyhoo Mountain plowed into his back and began blowing him across the ice. He was standing upright as the unrelenting winds carried him across the runway in the direction of the sea wall at the edge of the bay. Cameron could hardly believe it. As he accelerated ahead, he felt like he was wind-sailing. Eventually, he reached a ground speed he estimated to be close to twenty miles per hour. He asked himself, "Now, what do I do?"

Then the soles of Doug Cameron's flight boots hit a rough patch of ice, and he went tumbling.

"Doug got out of the aircraft first," recalls co-pilot Lt. Pat Bacher (pronounced "bah-shay"), "and he took like one or two steps, and the wind was blowing so hard, and the ramp was like a sheet of ice, and he just got under way! I was sitting in the cockpit, and I just look up and he just goes cooking across this ramp."

Bacher laughed at the strange and unexpected vision, and stepped cautiously from the copter. But, just as suddenly, he, too, was swept away by the amazing force of the wind. He ended up on the ground not far from where Doug Cameron lay. Cameron had felt a little embarrassed at having taken such an unexpected journey when, out of the corner of his eye, he caught sight of Bacher lying prostrate on the ice nearby. Bacher would recall how Cameron looked at him "with that smirk of his, and kind of chuckling, as if to say, 'Yeah, you were laughing at me, wise guy! So, *now* what do you have to say?'"

Later, inside the airport hangar, Pat Bacher found himself standing next to Aaron Bean. Bean knew Bacher had three youngsters back home in Kodiak and, with the Christmas season now in full swing, he turned to the officer.

"So, what do your kids want for Christmas?" he asked. "They want their daddy home alive."

With their H-60 fully fueled and ready for flight, Dave Neel and his crew paused to eat a bite of lunch. It was then that Neel received a call on his cell phone from headquarters ordering them back into the air. They were to launch immediately. In an effort to reclaim some cabin space for the rescue at hand, however, before departing they hurriedly removed everything from the H-60's rear cabin that was not tied down or bolted in.

As they prepared for takeoff, a snow squall pushed through, packing long and frenzied flurries, completely hiding the mountains from sight. The rescue scene was only fifteen miles away as a crow flies, just an eight-minute flight on a clear day, but with the steep, mountainous terrain standing thousands of feet high directly in their path, and heavy icing awaiting them at three hundred feet and above, they would be unable to fly directly to the scene. Neel and Watson would have to take the long way back to the freighter, a fifty-minute journey around the backside of the mountains, flying low across the water.

Switching positions in the H-60's cockpit, Doug Watson climbed into the right-side pilot's seat, strapped himself in, and lifted off. Heading north then, he rose to three hundred feet. Flying almost blindly, he made a left-hand turn at Cape Cheerful and, bordering the backside of Unalaska Island, headed out over open water.

In no time at all, snow flurries closed in on them, and their ability to see dropped to zero. Flying in the lee of the mountain range as they were, Doug Watson found himself accosted by "just ungodly" amounts of air turbulence, "with severe yaw-kicks," and he was obliged to notch it back a bit. Then, quite abruptly, CG6020 lost all communications with the outside world. Undeterred, Watson pressed on.

As far as piloting skills, abilities, and the kind of sound judgment that must accompany a pilot on patrol in Alaska went, Watson and Neel trusted each other completely. Dave Neel was considered one of the top pilots at Air Station Kodiak. He was, in fact, often referred to as "the ace of the base."

Though Neel loved flying, he also knew that Doug Watson was a certified instructor and a very capable aviator. They'd flown together on scores of missions out of Clearwater, Florida, and he had every confidence in his capabilities in the air. As a result, Neel felt his own talents would best be put to use in the left co-pilot's seat as the commanding officer and chief navigator on board. He'd be responsible for plotting their waypoints and for managing the mission.

Neel and Watson broke free of their communications blackout behind Unalaska Island and motored out across the angry, fitful face of the ocean. They were searching for both the cutter *Alex Haley* and the *Selendang Ayu*. But in the midst of the gleaming white of the breaking waves, with the big, wind-whipped seas randomly merging and diverging and breaking, the 273-foot-long cutter and the 738-foot-long freighter proved surprisingly difficult to spot.

"Is that the *Alex Haley* out there, Doug?" asked Neel.

"That kind of looks like it," replied Watson.

Scanning the seas and islands off to his left, Neel spotted the *Selendang Ayu*. The giant freighter was clearly dead in the water. Huge yet powerless, the vessel was only a few short miles from Skan Bay on Unalaska Island, and the rock-studded reefs and cliff-lined shores awaiting it there. Storm waves could be seen exploding along the entire length of her hull. Lying with her port side exposed to the blustery winds, she was rolling as much as thirty-five degrees in her side-to-side gyrations. And as she drifted along, twenty-five-foot breakers could be seen crashing over her deck and scouring it clean.

Behind it, the steep, treeless, desolate-looking slopes of Unalaska Island lay hidden under a coating of winter snow. The intimidating hunk of volcanic wilderness rose abruptly from the cliff tops at the water's edge, and ascended sharply in slopes that rose for more than three thousand feet into the broad, glacial fields that covered that high mountain terrain. The stark, black-and-white mixture of bare rock showing through the blowing snow and ground ice gave a bleak and unforgiving look to the landscape.

The vessel was "nowhere near" where Dave Neel had expected to find her. The ship was drifting steadily on toward Unalaska Island, at the mercy of the sea, at a speed of about 2 knots, with the *Alex Haley* running alongside her, still trying to make the save. If they didn't get a line on the freighter within the next hour or two, she'd surely run aground.

Oh my God, Neel mused silently to himself. *This situation is much worse than I'd imagined.* He turned to Doug Watson. "This ship is a lot closer to the shore than I ever expected."

Neel called on CB Channel 21 to inform the *Alex Haley* that the 6020 was now on scene.

"Stand by," came the reply. "We are in the process of trying to pass a towline."

TWO

Only minutes after daybreak, at approximately 10:30 A.M., during one of the shortest days of the year in Alaska, Cdr. Matt Bell, captain of the CG cutter *Alex Haley,* decided to try to take the *Selendang Ayu* in tow. He had reason to be confident in the *Alex Haley*'s abilities.

Built by the Navy, in 1948, and named the U.S.S. *Edenton*, this ship was later recommissioned by the Coast Guard and rechristened (in 1999) in honor of the author of *Roots.* She had once, single-handedly towed the sixty-thousand-ton battleship *Wisconsin* and her impressive array of fourteen cannons into a safe harbor. The cutter came with a flying bridge that extended out from the port side of the wheelhouse, thirty-six feet above the sea. It was built that way to allow her captain a clear line of sight both fore and aft. Cdr. Bell's decisions as master of the ship were generally made inside the vessel's wheelhouse, which stands about sixty feet back from her bow.

When she came into the possession of the Coast Guard, they slapped a helicopter flight deck and hangar on her stern. Quite unlike the single-engine, single-propeller system that had so completely failed the *Selendang Ayu*, the *Alex Haley* has a propulsion system that includes four large diesel engines and four similarly powered generators that provide energy and thrust to two brass, ten-foot-wide, controllable-pitch propellers.

Most important—especially when navigating in high seas—is the way she was built. Capable as they are, standard cutters such as the *Munro* and the *Rush* are 378 feet long, 36 feet wide, and require a crew of 170 when under way. The *Alex Haley*, on the other hand, is just 283 feet long. But being a full 40 feet in width, she is significantly more stable, and needs only 100 sailors to sail her, though it would still cost something on the order of $200 million to replace her.

Cdr. Bell initiated the present rescue attempt by steering the *Alex Haley* upwind of the giant, heaving ship. Bell had come to believe that it was probably their last chance to intercept the disabled vessel. Giving it his best shot, he "ran past it," he recalls, "then turned around and came back, running into the wind and seas. You could see the guys standing on top of the fo'c'sle. I was on the bridge, and when I looked up I saw four members of the *Selendang Ayu* up there waiting to catch our line.

"Our gunner's mate stood on our flight deck [on the *Alex Haley*'s stern]. Using a line-throwing gun, he shot the line across. It was spectacular, the most perfect shot I've ever seen, straight up over the bow. He split the four men standing on the fo'c'sle right down the middle, and they were able to grab the shot line. You couldn't have scripted it any better."

Steve Schmid, a crewman on the flight deck of the *Alex Haley*, recalls that he was close enough to actually hear the "monkey's fist"—that rock-hard, baseball-sized knot of ropeline spliced on the end of the messenger line—strike the metal deck of the freighter.

"Then the guys up there on the fo'c'sle tried to haul this line in," recalls Bell. "But of course, it's just that thin, orange, parachute cord–sized line. They pulled on that messenger line, and finally got to the thicker, heavier line attached to it." And as the weight of the eight-inch hauser, the actual towline itself, came to bear upon them, the speed of their efforts slowed noticeably.

"I'm out on the bridge way," adds Cdr. Bell, "asking my OD to slow down, and trying to talk to my X/O. He was standing several hundred feet away on the rear flight deck watching the folks working with the line. We're barely making way. And just as we start to slow down—BOOM!—the first big wave strikes!

"And now we've turned to starboard, and are running completely beam-to the oncoming seas. We're going in the opposite direction as the *Selendang Ayu*, and those guys on the deck of the freighter above me are trying to pull about a hundred yards' worth of that same huge hauser line up on their bow deck, fifty feet in the air. Impossible!"

Standing on the wind wing, exposed to the full force of the wind, Cdr. Bell glanced up in time to see the frail-looking, 5/8-inch messenger line suddenly part, and the megathick hauser line attached to it fall limply into the sea just off the *Alex Haley's* stern. Bell immediately disengaged the cutter's propellers and drifted for a time as the line washed around in the swirl of the ship's residual prop wash.

Bell knew there was no way he could reengage his ship's propellers without immediately getting that same towline entangled in them. Such a move would seize up both propellers in only seconds, with no way to clear them. Then it'd be "game over." But now, with all forward motion halted, the ship quickly began to lose steerage, and with the winds whipping up and pushing him toward shore, the *Alex Haley* began to drift sideways into the bludgeoning form of the *Selendang Ayu's* freewheeling bow.

The notion of being slammed on the rocks right along

with the *Selendang Ayu* and placing the *Alex Haley*'s one hundred men and women in harm's way was unthinkable. With no way to maintain steerage, Cdr. Bell would soon be forced to order the cutter's anchor be dropped as well, at least long enough for his crew to somehow extract the line from her props.

Observing from the flying bridge, Cdr. Bell studied the movements of the towline in the water, while simultaneously keeping an ear tuned to the sounds of the VHS radio chatter drifting out the side door of the wheelhouse. But in no time, it seemed, the *Alex Haley* drifted in so close to the *Selendang Ayu* that Bell felt he could have almost "reached out and touched it."

"So I've got a nasty tail," he recalls, "and an eight-inch-thick hauser hanging behind me. And I swear it's going to get wrapped up in our screws and, in about two seconds, we'd be *done!* But several bosun's mates are back there on the stern with axes trying to chop through it.

"So I started talking to myself. I have a tendency to do that when I'm watching evolutions. When other people hear what I'm saying, they know what I'm thinking. And I'm saying, 'Wow, this is going bad really quickly. We need to get out of here. Those guys are *never* going to be able to pull that hauser line up there. It's just too darned heavy. We're going to have to pass that line up to them again. Here we are, beam-to [sideways to the onslaught of incoming seas], and we've got a nasty tail hanging off our stern . . .'"

Simultaneously, as he spoke, Cdr. Bell could hear his X/O Phil Thorne screaming on the radio, "Cut the line! Cut the line!"

"They finally chopped through it," says Bell. "And what was hanging over our fantail got swept away."

Then Cdr. Bell turned and shouted to his officer of the deck, "Okay, OD! We need to get out of here! So get us out of here NOW!"

"Helmsman!" said the OD. "Right full rudder! All ahead full at forty PSI [pounds per square inch]!"

At that moment, Cdr. Bell felt lucky to have two ten-foot propellers and as many engines capable of powering them out of the turn. And he thought to himself, *Engines, please don't fail me now!*

They "put the torque on the wheel," adds Bell, and gave the ship a "big, huge, hard rudder to get back up into the swell, and we began moving safely ahead again."

At one point, the *Sidney Foss* succeeded in getting a towline over to the *Selendang Ayu.* Those in the wheelhouse of the *Alex Haley* watched as the tugboat tried repeatedly to take control of her and begin the tow, but they never were able to turn the ship into the wind, not even close, and when the tow parted "we were watching," adds Cdr. Bell.

Later, Cdr. Bell radioed the captain of the *Sidney Foss,*

asking if they were going to "redo the tow." The captain replied that with their stern awash in such gargantuan seas, there was no way for his people to work safely on deck. Under such impossible conditions, they wouldn't be able to make the tow happen.

Bell knew the captain of the *Sidney Foss* was right. "The tugboat's stern was completely awash. If one of his deckhands were to get swept overboard, he'd never have seen him again."

Also on board the *Alex Haley* were pilots Lt. Tim Eason and Lt. Rob Kornexl. Eason was born and raised in beautiful Savannah, Georgia, an historic town "with a charm all its own." As a graduate of the University of Georgia, and a hardcore Bulldog football fan, Eason enlisted in the Coast Guard when he was just twenty-three years old.

At ease among the bright and the disciplined, yet possessing the common touch as well, Eason was eventually sent back to Washington, D.C., and assigned to the the Armed Forces Inaugural Committee—a group whose function is to help plan the ceremonies surrounding the swearing in of each new president. A graduate of OCS, and the flight school in Pensacola, Florida, he served a four-year stretch flying missions out of New Orleans before being assigned to Air Station Kodiak and his present duties patroling the tempestuous waters of the Bering Sea.

Good weather or bad, Eason loved the challenging and unpredictable nature of flying in Alaska. He had a sharp, heads-up crew who got along quite well. This latest patrol, however, had been a particularly arduous one aboard the *Alex Haley*. Throughout the month of November, and well into December, they "pretty much got [their] butts kicked" by Alaska's tenacious weather.

They'd ridden out a series of winter storms packing big seas and fierce winds. The weather was so rough that they'd gone twelve consecutive days without being able to fly. Tours like this left flight-loving aviators like Eason feeling as though they were trapped aboard a floating prison, with the ever-present danger of drowning.

They were about ready to motor home to Kodiak, when the *Alex Haley* was "diverted to assist" in this latest high-seas drama. Upon first impression, however, it really didn't sound like much of a mission. The disappointment on board ship was unmistakable. "That's just great!" ran the sentiment. "Here we have to go and play nursemaid to some broken ship. This mission could go on for days. We sure as hell won't be getting home on schedule, now."

Thirty-three-year-old Rob Kornexl, Eason's fellow pilot and comrade in the current search and rescue mission, had been brought up in the dairy farming region of northern

Michigan. A trim, active runner and bicyclist, he stands five feet eight and weighs about 160 pounds.

Kornexl had flown some ten years of hard core combat-related helicopter missions for the Army, before opting out. He lived as a civilian for a couple of months, then decided to join the Coast Guard. He and his Air Force wife Kerrie wanted to raise a family. "We wanted to have kids," he says. "We were looking for the best quality of life we could have for our children, while still continuing to serve our country. The Coast Guard seemed like a good compromise."

Following a four-year tour of duty in Detroit, Michigan, the Kornexls signed on to go to Alaska. Not everyone who moves to Kodiak Island takes to the no-nonsense nature of life there. But as it turned out, Rob Kornexl and his wife "absolutely loved the place." Arriving there in June of 2002, they took to the tightly knit, small-town nature of the community, while embracing the fishing-hunting-hiking type of outdoor activities the area offers.

Now, two and a half years later, with a solid background in wilderness flying to add to an already prodigious body of flight experience, veteran pilots Rob Kornexl—with over three thousand hours—and Tim Eason—with more than two thousand hours—were about to be drawn into one of the most demanding, deadliest, no-holds-barred rescue missions in Alaskan history.

■   ■   ■

Characteristic of SAR pilots, Eason and Kornexl were itching to get their H-65 Dolphin helicopter airborne and into the action. However, stuck as they were on board the *Alex Haley,* they were faced with one apparently insurmountable obstacle: the maximum allowable limits for standard launches from Coast Guard cutters while under way are five degrees pitch and seven degrees roll. It was a standard which was virtually never circumvented.

Outside, however, their flight deck was currently pitching fifteen degrees, and rolling twenty, "both plus and minus." As the cutter continued to leap and dive beneath them, staggering along through the present sea state, they knew that Cdr. Bell probably wouldn't allow it.

Regardless, Eason and Kornexl discussed at length the idea of getting their H-65 airborne, as well as the prospects of attempting a "heavy weather traverse," with both Cdr. Bell and flight deck crew boss Dale Estilette. If they were somehow called into the action, they would use the smaller H-65 to evacuate the twenty-six sailors from the drifting freighter, a few at a time. They'd set up a land-based rescue operation in which they would shuttle the men to shore, and then sprint back to the ship for more.

Eason and Kornexl were raring to go. They approached Cdr. Bell in the wheelhouse.

"Sir, we need to get into this," Tim Eason suggested. "We need to fly for this."

"In this weather?" countered Cdr. Bell, warily studying the thirty-foot seas and green water starting to break over the *Alex Haley*'s bow. "Tim, it's awfully rough out."

Just to humor them, Cdr. Bell invited Eason and Kornexl to step outside to see for themselves. Squinting into the fierce, cold winds Kornexl, Eason, and Bell made their way out onto the flying bridge, and stood there studying the scene as the ominous-looking storm waves lumbered by on either side of the ship.

"All right, now!" called out Bell, notching his voice up an octave to be heard. "Take a look at it out here. Let's think this through. What would it be like if we really had to do this? If we *had* to, could we get you into the air? Because this is what it would look like."

As they watched, "two or three of the big rollers would come by and basically take us out of parameters," recalls Cdr. Bell. "But then that fourth or fifth wave would be a really big one, and we would ride it down into the trough and then all the way to the top. The waves were so big that we would just sit up there on top for a few seconds, and the deck would stay fairly level. That looked to be a pilot's only window of opportunity."

Cdr. Bell completely understood their frustrations. The truth was that there was no way he and his crew could carry out their patrols and rescue missions without such dedicated aviators. Secretly, however, Cdr. Bell knew that all of this was just academic. With two of the powerhouse H-60 Jayhawk helicopters and their crews already on scene, there was no way the comparatively pint-sized H-65 would be called into duty.

But here I am, he thought, *with these extremely capable pilots who are willing to risk everything to save these sailors . . . but I can't allow them to fly off my deck."*

"You're not going," Cdr. Bell said finally. "There's just no way."

One of the difficulties in dealing with the captain of another ship, Cdr. Bell knew, was that he did not have the right to tell that captain what to do. For better or worse, he was "still the master of his vessel." Legally, Captain Kailash Bhushan Singh was completely within his rights. According to maritime law, the master of a commercial freighter under way on the high seas virtually anywhere in the world has the authority to make decisions as he sees fit, regardless of the apparent dangers to his men presented by the environment. Once the *Selendang Ayu* put out to sea, it became Singh's ship, his cargo, and his crew.

At the same time, as the senior officer on board the *Alex Haley* it was Cdr. Bell's responsibility to actively engage the skipper of the *Selendang Ayu* over the radio and try to convince him to begin releasing his people, so they could start hoisting them. But the captain from India would have none of it. He was apparently convinced that he and his engineers would soon fix the problem and be on their way.

Although he had never met the captain of the disabled freighter—about whom he was, even now, receiving only fragmented pieces of information—Mr. Singh had over thirty years of oceangoing experience under his belt. And while he possessed an unlimited master's license, it was only the second time he had crossed the Bering Sea.

Cdr. Bell could feel for him. Here was a man, Bell was convinced, who was probably down in the wildly gyrating space of his ship's engine room at that moment, working right alongside the vessel's engineers, trying to fix his engine. At any second, he thinks he's going to get his main engine back online, and get shuck of the whole impossible mess. He'll just drive away then, and never look back.

As the freighter drew closer to the shoreline, and the water began to shallow up, Cdr. Bell suggested to the *Selendang Ayu*'s skipper that he lower one of its anchors. That would at least slow its motion toward the beach. *If he gets his anchor down*, Bell thought, *that might buy us a little more time.*

The captain of the *Selendang Ayu* accepted Cdr. Bell's suggestion, and soon dropped his port-side anchor. To everyone's surprise, the vessel did actually fetch up. The ship pivoted around and, with its bow pointing into the wind, began riding up and over the rising groundswells. Cdr. Bell considered pulling alongside the ship and trying to pass another towline to her, but with the seas rolling in the way they were, he quickly nixed the idea.

One of Cdr. Bell's worst fears, however, was quickly born out when the *Selendang Ayu*'s port-side anchor began to slip. The *Alex Haley*'s radar clearly showed the vessel sliding ever closer to the reef-laden shallows.

Once again, Cdr. Bell radioed the ship's captain. "Okay, Captain," he began. "Now we *really* need to start thinking about taking some of your people off! If we can hoist some of your folks off right now, that would leave us fewer to worry about later, if your ship actually does run aground."

The freighter's captain acknowledged that Cdr. Bell was probably correct. But, once again, the discussion seemed to stall right there.

"If I let you take some off of ship," the captain finally replied, "will you put them back on later?"

"Oh, sure," countered Cdr. Bell, tongue in cheek. "We'll put them back on first thing tomorrow morning."

"So here we are now," recalls Bell, "at a point where we're trying to figure out what we're going to do."

All parties were hoping that, at any moment, the *Selendang Ayu*'s anchor would snag on the ocean floor and hold her there long enough for them "to establish a tow," as Bell explains, "or they'd get their engine fixed and it will be 'game over,' as they say." But then, without warning, the port-side anchor chain parted, releasing the giant bulk carrier to the mercy of the wind and seas.

THREE

With his vessel in imminent danger of running aground, the ship's captain agreed to begin releasing his crew. Still airborne in their H-60 and waiting for those survivors to appear on deck, veteran pilots Dave Neel and Doug Watson remained doubtful.

When, once again, no one appeared on deck, Neel turned to Watson.

"Hey, Doug," he said. "Let's go take another look at the best place to hoist these folks from."

Again, they began staggering across the sky around the large vessel, ready at a moment's notice to move into position to begin the hoisting evolutions. As they waited, they took in the sobering vision of mountainous waves breaking along the full length of her port side. The gleaming white avalanches of water exploded off the fifty-foot-wide, eight-foot-high cargo holds that lined the pivoting surface of her deck. Tendrils of mist rose from the accelerating deluge, and were whisked away by the eviscerating winds, blown out across the ragged, silvery-gray face of the sea.

The incalculable tonnage of the thick-bodied combers pounding across her midships and filling the deck pushed the already wild, side-to-side motions of the vessel to levels so violent, it looked almost out of control.

The freighter's wheelhouse was as tall and wide as a six-story apartment complex. The tiny, square windows of individual staterooms etched into its tall, broad face looked out over a sprawling arena of deck that was nearly twice the length of a football field, and fourteen feet wider than that of the *Titanic*.

Staggered down the middle of the deck, in the relatively narrow gaps between the rectangular-shaped cargo holds, stood four giant steel crane towers. These chunky, round steel stanchions were about twelve feet in diameter, and rose to a height of nearly sixty feet above the deck. Each time a wave spilled over the side of the ship, a threatening river of foamy sea would bleed off the hold covers. Then it would begin jetting through the narrow, trenchlike spaces between those holds, flooding around the bases of the towers like the white water a river becomes when it is squeezed between narrow canyon walls.

Extending out horizontally over the holds and deck from the base of each of the towers was a long, steel boom arm, about fifty feet long. This boom could be moved up and down and right and left to facilitate both loading and offloading of various products, and was controlled by an array of steel cables that swooped down from the top of the crane like the suspension cables on the Golden Gate Bridge. Locked solidly in place, these four booms were used to remove the hold covers, and to assist in the transfer of cargo—in this case, sixty-one thousand metric tons of soybeans—to and from the vessel.

The center hatch cover in the middle of the ship had a large *H* painted on it. At first glance, that appeared to be the likeliest location from which to perform the rescue.

"Doug," declared Neel to his partner. "Let's do a dry run right there, just to see what this is going to look like."

Watson swung in on a low approach. Riding beam-to the oncoming seas, the giant ship continued to drift through the steep, ocean swells. Also plainly visible was the threat posed by the runaway deck wash. Directly in front of them now, a storm wave caught the port-side edge of the ship at the lowest, teetering point of its roll, and, remarkably, powered aboard almost intact. Twenty feet of frothy sea tore across the open deck.

Both pilots found the sight unsettling. Any person caught trying to make his way across the midships to be hoisted stood a good chance of being crushed against the cargo hold covers, or carried away and mangled—if not dismembered outright—as they were washed through the steel bars of the four-foot-high hand railings on the downslope side of the deck. Broken, helpless, they'd be carried overboard, lost forever.

Equally intimidating was the sight of the cranes, cables, and long steel boom arms sweeping back and forth, making any attempts to hoist from the center of the deck perilous, if not altogether impossible.

This isn't going to work, thought Neel.

As the *Selendang Ayu* drifted steadily on, and the distance between it and the shore shrank, the lives of those who remained on board were becoming increasingly imperiled. Both pilots could see it all unfolding right below them. What mystified them was how the ship's captain could not. Could he still be holding onto the belief that he was about to get his main engine restarted? So far, and in spite of all his promises, he had yet to release any of his crew to be airlifted. His inaction was eating up precious time, and forcing everyone, both in the air and on board the foundering freighter, into an ever more dangerous predicament.

■   ■   ■

The *Alex Haley*'s flight deck crew boss Dale Estilette (pronounced "ess-tell-let") had been born in Morgan City in the bayous of the southern portion of Louisiana. He was just eighteen when he first went to work as a rough-neck on the offshore oil drilling rigs in the Gulf of Mexico that lay virtually in his backyard. After six years of dangerous, sweat-filled labor, he quit the rigs to begin a career in the U.S. Coast Guard. Now, with some twenty-two years of adventure and work experience under his belt, Estilette had assimilated a lot along the way. Most important, he'd learned how to perform difficult and dangerous tasks safely, while working with crews of men and women in a rugged and unpredictable marine environment.

His father, too, had worked as a roughneck laborer and foreman in those same oil fields off the coast of Louisiana for almost fifty years. Estilette learned a lot from him, a man he both loved and respected. Along the way, his father had taught him "how to treat people, and get them to work for you," says Estilette. He believed that one had to "earn their respect, to get their respect." It was a kind of working man's Golden Rule. "Do for them, as you would have them do for you."

Just a few months before, the forty-year-old Estilette was engaged in another two-month patrol of the Bering Sea, the seventeenth of his career, when he received word that his father had unexpectedly died.

That said, Dale Estilette—and the wisdom that his father had passed onto him—were now living on aboard the cutter *Alex Haley,* with Estilette engaging as a key player in what would prove to be the most dramatic rescue mission of his Coast Guard career.

When the *Alex Haley* was first diverted to assist a freighter that had lost its power, Estilette wondered at the news. The 11,500-horsepower diesel engine that normally powered such a ship was "about the size of a house." He knew that if the mechanics on board the *Selendang Ayu* were experienced enough, they could actually shut down an individual piston and crawl inside its sleeve to make most repairs while the motor was still running. But word had it that for some unknown reason they'd shut down the entire engine and were unable, now, to get it restarted.

Outside, fierce williwaws were staggering all those who dared to venture out on deck. The seas were twenty-five feet sustained, with much larger rogues forming, and the storm clearly intensifying. Dale Estilette understood perfectly what helicopter pilots and their crews were experiencing out there. Over the years, he'd launched out on countless rescue missions aboard H-60 Jayhawk helicopters as a flight mechanic.

During one particular mission on a cold January night back in 1996, Estilette's crew had received a mayday call from the skipper of a king crab boat that was sinking fast in the Bering Sea. It was pitch dark out. The last word they had was that the fishermen were all in survival suits, and were abandoning ship. Then the radio signal went dead. They immediately launched the H-60.

It was a clear but windy night, and traveling at 180 miles per hour, the stars shone brightly against the blue-black canopy of heaven. As they hurried along, Estilette could make out the soft, mastlight glow of other fishing vessels working beyond the horizon. Some of those same boats were already steaming toward their shipwrecked comrades, but with a top speed of eight or nine knots, as they navigated through close-cropped seas, it would take them several hours to reach the search area.

Arriving on scene, Estilette's copter slowed to a hover above an island of flotsam, oil, and debris floating on the surface. Estilette slid the side door open and kneeled in the doorway as they searched for survivors. They spotted only one, and quickly hoisted him aboard.

"How many more are there?" Estilette yelled, pressing the hypothermic crewman for more information.

"There are four more of us," he stammered. "They're all wearing survival suits. They're in the water somewhere around here."

Racing back and forth across the water, Estilette and his crewmates searched the darkness. Eventually, they managed to locate all of the missing fishermen, hoisting each to safety. "That was five lives saved," he recalls, understandably pleased to have played a part in it.

Inside the wheelhouse of the *Alex Haley,* Cdr. Matt Bell and his staff continued in the command role, making all calls and decisions for Coast Guard personnel on scene. He was still trying to get the captain of the *Selendang Ayu* to make good on his promise and begin releasing his people, but so far, without luck.

Scouting it out as he went, Doug Watson flew the H-60 Jayhawk along the full length of the tossing freighter in search of a suitable hoisting area. Maneuvering downwind of the vessel, he made another pass over her stern. Nothing looked acceptable. There was a fairly large opening between two hatch covers in the middle of the deck, but they had already been there, and had written that off. Besides, the freighter was rocking back and forth far too violently. The tall steel towers looked like giant metronome arms, just waiting to swat them from the sky.

"How am I going to do this?" puzzled Watson, what with the boat pitching up and down, and rolling about, and the waves crashing across the deck. As he watched, another breaker swept up onto the port side, exploded over the cargo holds, and thundered across the deck. The bow of the *Selendang Ayu* dipped low, and then slowly began to rise. As it did, waist-deep seawater drained off the tops of her cargo holds, down the deck, and poured over the side, giving the ship the appearance of a submarine rising.

"Hey," Neel said to Watson. "Let's go check out the bow area. That's usually more stable."

Making their way forward, they studied the forty-foot-high steel mast mounted in the center of the elevated bow deck. That would present a problem, but nothing like that posed by the four tall cranes standing bolt upright and aligned along the entire length of the vessel's main deck. The bow, they soon agreed, looked to be their best chance for success. By paralleling the ship's movements, Doug Watson hoped to hover in close and hoist low over the area.

Though far from the comparative safety inside the dry, upper floors of the freighter's wheelhouse, the fo'c'sle area—directly behind and about eight feet below the elevated bow deck—looked like it just might provide a bit of protection from the wind and weather for those waiting to be airlifted.

Then, in the distance, Dave Neel spotted an ominous-looking island of blizzard snow advancing across the water. The color, movement, and force behind it was "mesmerizing." Tearing at the edges of the dark gray storm cell were several small, tornado-shaped formations—swirling vortices of windblown destruction sliding steadily across the face of the sea.

As the snow squall rolled through, it reduced visibility to about one-eighth of a mile. Like the others, however, once it had passed, "it would clear up and be beautiful, other than the wind," recalls Neel. "Then twenty minutes later, another snow squall would come rolling through and do the same thing all over again."

Since the captain of the *Selendang Ayu* had first agreed, at least in principle, to start releasing his people, more than an hour had clicked past. Then another thirty minutes passed, and still no one appeared. Captain Singh deflected further Coast Guard inquiries with continued assurances that the crewmen on his ship were still making preparations to leave.

"We need to start preparing a contingency plan here," said Dave Neel. "Because if this ship goes ashore and breaks up right here, we're not going to have enough time to ferry loads of survivors the forty-five minutes each way to Dutch Harbor, and get back on-scene again before this ship goes down."

"Doug," said Neel to Watson, "let's go scout out the shoreline over there and see if we can't find a place where we can ferry people to. We need to find a place where we can leave them for a little while, where they'll be safe, so we can go back and rescue the rest. We need to get all twenty-six of those crewmen off that ship before it sinks. Then we can deal with transporting them into Dutch Harbor."

Doug Watson agreed. The jagged rock ridges and mountainous terrain jutting out of the sea and ascending into the snow fields high above looked so overwhelmingly large they were intimidating. Mile upon mile of the craggy shoreline—ringed with tall, black rows of volcanic cliffs—greeted anyone coming ashore. However, there did appear to be a promising stetch of land several miles farther up the coastline. Watson was moving ahead to check it out, when an invisible downdraft of mountain air tumbled off the cliff tops, wrapped itself around the terrain, and very nearly planted them in the ground—helicopter, flight crew, and all.

Recovering from that unexpected encounter, Watson finally came upon a suitable landing area. But when they flew back to the *Selendang Ayu,* there were still no survivors waiting out on deck and they were forced, once again, to wait and circle, burning up their precious—and quite finite—supply of fuel.

Eventually, one crewman appeared on deck, but when they hovered in closer to initiate the hoist, he disappeared inside a door leading into the fo'c'sle. "A few minutes later," recalls Dave Neel, "he came back out, looked at us, and then went back in again. He repeated this for the next fifteen minutes. Then another guy came out, looked at us, and went back inside."

All the while, the voice from Command Center on the *Alex Haley* continued to urge the captain to step forward and help initiate the rescue. "Hey, we need to get going, now, Captain," said Cdr. Bell. "Time's a-wasting!"

Neel and Watson were still anxiously waiting for Captain Singh to start releasing members of his crew, when they heard him announce to the *Alex Haley* that he intended to lower his second and last anchor. During the night, Neel knew, the captain had dropped his port-side anchor, but it had eventually sheered off. There was nothing left now but the stub end of its chain hanging down.

Finally, three crewmen walked out from the fo'c'sle compartment, lifting Watson's hopes. Without communicating their intent, they hurried over to the starboard side and gathered around the anchor winch. As the ship continued to leap and roll, they worked the release mechanisms and soon managed to drop the starboard anchor over the side.

All parties looked on in anticipation, as the freighter's second anchor chain rattled overboard. Soon thereafter, with the anchor now sitting solidly on the bottom, the ship began to swing around, with her bow pointing, more or less, into the wind. She looked to be riding in a far more stable fashion.

Up until that time, Watson and his crew aboard the H-60 were "cussing them pretty good for wasting our time and using up our fuel."

Dave Neel radioed the *Alex Haley* with the good news.

"Hey, I think it *is* helping," he said. "I believe their anchor is grabbing!"

The *Selendang Ayu*'s captain was quick to agree. "Yes!" he radioed. "I think it is working!"

Disappointingly, those tracking the *Selendang Ayu* on the *Alex Haley*'s radar soon detected that the freighter was continuing to drift closer to shore. The second anchor was apparently also being dragged across the ocean floor, slowing, but not stopping, the vessel's agonizing slide. Cdr. Bell informed Captain Singh of that fact. The sailors aboard his ship needed to be removed from the vessel forthwith!

Hoisting twenty-six sailors off the leaping, plunging forepeak of so large a vessel in such wicked seas and winds would be exceptionally challenging. Moving in top-to-bottom swings of as much as fifty feet, the soaring, diving bow of the *Selendang Ayu* posed an aeronautical challenge all its own. Doug Watson hovered in closer to observe it. The successive eruptions of pummeling waves and pitching vessel were daunting. He knew in a glance that no cable winch or flight mech would be able to compensate for such extreme fluctuations. It'd be enough of a challenge, in such battering winds, to get the rescue basket anywhere near the target.

Watson could easily imagine the bow springing into the sky, and then free-falling into the sea, just as a nasty gust of wind sent his helicopter careening. The whiplash of cable and basket might well break the rider's back.

Regardless of the bow's extreme motion, Doug Watson made the calculated decision to fly in formation with it. Moving along in tandem, when the bow rose, he, too, would rise. And when the bow went into a free fall, he would mimic the plummeting motion, and descend right along with it. It was a sound plan, theoretically.

As the *Selendang Ayu* drifted ever closer to the rocky shoals of Unalaska Island the tension among the Coast Guard ranks, both in the air and on the sea, intensified. Finally, Dave Neel radioed the *Alex Haley*, and asked Cdr. Bell for permission to speak directly to the freighter's captain. Having received the go-ahead, Neel tried to set him straight.

"Sir," Neel began, "you don't need twenty-six people on board your vessel there to help you restart your engine, do you? So how about letting some of your folks off?"

Though the captain spoke somewhat understandable English, Neel suspected that he didn't necessarily comprehend it very well. Speaking in very plain language, he briefed the man on "what we were going to do, where we planned to hoist from, and what his people needed to be prepared for."

Once again, the captain agreed. Prepared to hoist at a

moment's notice, Watson "waited and waited and waited, and kept looking for his people," but no one appeared.

This hoisting operation would be far from routine. Moving in closer, Doug Watson studied the *Selendang Ayu*'s bow soaring into the sky right in front of him. As the rise and fall of the bow became ever more energized by the rhythm of the oncoming waves, the large, round speed-enhancing bulb welded to the freighter's bow leapt clear of the sea.

Normally submerged while under way, the massive, red, torpedo-shaped nose of the vessel soared high into the sky, now, spewing silver volleys of ocean spray. Then, plunging straight down, it disappeared into the depths, before rebounding once again. Watson could see "parts of the bow you would see only if she was in dry dock."

At long last, a few stragglers began to wander out on deck. Each wore one of the old-type, "big, orange, foam-block life preservers" over slacks, button-down shirts, and pullover sweaters—the kind of clothes one might wear to dinner in town. Doug Watson wasted no time. Hovering over the hoisting area on the port side of the bouncing freighter, he began flying in tandem again, just as he had planned, moving along as precisely as he could, paralleling the rise and fall of her bow.

Brian Lickfield rushed the rescue basket down and watched dumbfounded as one of the crewman threw his suitcase inside it, and stepped back. It was as if he thought those fighting to hold position and fly in formation overhead were running some kind of elevator service. Lickfield's first winch was, in fact, a suitcase hoist. The experience left him "thoroughly pissed." On the next evolution, the same crewman climbed into the basket and Lickfield boomed him up.

Dave Neel could feel the lack of love. So he called Captain Singh and informed him that he was there to hoist the captain and his crew to safety, not their luggage.

During yet another full hour of prompting and urging and waiting, more members of the *Selendang Ayu*'s crew made their appearances. It was clear to those hovering in the rarified air overhead that no one on the deck below was taking charge. The freighter's crewmen continued to move toward the hoisting area with little sense of urgency, and in a manner that seemed completely oblivious to the extreme risks the Coasties were taking, being forced, as they were, to hover in such an exposed and compromising position. The behavior of the sailors below was unconscionable; their attitude, almost cavalier.

It was a painful experience for the pilots and crew of the H-60, "hovering up there in the air that long," being so far from the nearest airport and knowing that they would soon run so low on fuel that they'd be forced to abandon the effort and return to base.

"Oh, man, are these guys ever slow," thought rescue swimmer Aaron Bean. "We came to save you. So come on now, just get in the damned basket!"

But no one could seem to instill upon the ship's captain or its crew the proper sense of urgency. And while both Lt. Dave Neel and Cdr. Matt Bell took turns trying to convince Captain Singh that he and his ship were about to run aground, and that his time had run out, individual members of his twenty-six-man crew continued to come slowly trickling out, scattered and disheveled, like sleepwalkers showing up late for breakfast.

FOUR

Once again, Doug Watson bellied up to the *Selendang Ayu*'s hoisting area, and Brian Lickfield guided his rescue basket down onto the deck, only to have another crewman from India begin filling it with his suitcase and personal belongings.

"Sir, that guy on deck down there just loaded up our rescue basket with luggage again," complained Lickfield. "That's a bunch of bullshit!"

Neel was still feeling compassionate at that point. In a tone of resignation, he replied, "Brian, bring up the luggage, and I'll call the captain."

"Sir," he began, in his radio address to the ship's

captain, "your people are still sending up baggage in the rescue basket, instead of climbing into it themselves."

"I tell them they can bring a personal bag," said the captain.

"Sir, we are out here to get your *people,* not their baggage!"

"Well, then you must be the one to tell them," said the captain.

"No," shot back Neel, the intensity in his voice rising fast now. "I'm up here in the helicopter. I have no way of communicating with them from up here. You are on the ship. You are their captain. *You* need to tell them!"

"Okay, okay, okay."

Occasionally, as he rode the winds aloft, Doug Watson would fly the chopper up and away from the freighter and stand off as the wind cells pelted them, in the hope that the storm winds might ease, or that more crew members would show up, or that the ship's captain or one of his officers would eventually man-up and expedite the process.

Instead, over the course of the next hour, crewmen on the giant freighter would poke their heads out the fo'c'sle door and stare up at him. Then they'd disappear back inside and close the door behind them, often never to be seen again. Others wandered out onto the wet, windblown deck, only to shuffle back inside again. No one on board the H-60 had ever seen anything quite like it.

With Watson at the controls flying into headwinds that seemed to be increasing by the hour, the position of the helicopter, in relation to the ship, held remarkably steady during the hoisting operations.

On the base back in Kodiak, Watson was known as one of the Coast Guard's most capable pilots. "He could do some amazing things with a helicopter," Aaron Bean notes with pride. "He could turn circles around most of the rest of the guys, because he had those controls *down!* I mean, he was the *man!*"

If so, Watson had joined the ranks of some extremely gifted aviators. Any such discussion should include the names of at least a few of those with nerves of steel and sound judgment, who flew on some of history's most famous Alaskan SAR cases—megatalented pilots such as Bill Adickes, Greg Breithaupt, Robert C. Powell, Tony Clark, Ted Lefeuvre, Jim Hatfield, Brian McLaughlin, Dan Molthen, Jimmy Ng, Mike Patterson, Tom Preston, Pat Rivas, Gene Rush, Paul Ratté, Robin Starrett, Jim Stiles, Malcolm Smith, Steve Bonn, Dave Durham, Matt Stanley, Mike Tanner, Steve Torpey, Shawn Tripp, John Whiddon, Bob "Chopper" Yerex, Russ Zullick, and the fearless one himself, Kodiak's very own Tom Walters.

With an impressive 4,200 hours of flying time to his credit, including numerous missions to the Bering Sea, co-pilot Lt. Dave Neel was also similarily touted. He knew a good deal about plucking hapless sailors off of bouncing ships out on the open sea. Just the year before, near Sand Point, at the base of the Aleutian Mountains, he'd hoisted an injured sailor off the tall, swaying superstructure of another freighter by flying backward—in the fog, at night.

Another time, in 2001, shortly after Neel first arrived in Kodiak, he found himself airborne at three in the morning in a hellacious storm south of Cordova. He and a pilot named Lt. Mike Tanner had been sent out on that god-awful night to try to rescue two fishermen off a ninety-foot salmon tender that was struggling in big seas in Prince William Sound. A tender is generally a king crab boat contracted during the summer months to pack salmon from far out on the fishing grounds to the cannery that hired them back in town.

"This tender," Neel recalls, "had lost its steerage and was about to run aground on Bligh Reef. It was very scary. We took off out of Cordova, and headed south, and you could not see out the front of the glass, the weather was so bad."

They were getting blown all over the sky. By using his NVGs (night-vision goggles), and looking out the left side of the helicopter, Neel could make out "these giant waves. I was new. It scared the shit out of me! It was so bad, we couldn't even land the rescue basket on the ship.

"Our gutsy rescue swimmer Tony Trout proposed a procedure to get the fishermen below that was extremely dangerous. Tony wanted to do a hoist where we hook him up and lower him down. Once in the water, he planned to disconnect from the cable and swim over to the survivors. And I said, 'Absolutely not! We're not going to do that. I don't want to end up having to save *three* people out here tonight, just the two.'

"So we did a direct swimmer deployment. We had the guys abandon ship [in survival suits] and jump into the sea. We kept Tony on the hoist cable, and he swam over to them, grabbed one, and held on tight. And our flight mech hauled them up that way, one survivor at a time."

"Captain!" Dave Neel radioed the captain of the *Selendang Ayu*. "We need to get some more people out here! We're waiting out here, burning up our precious fuel. We need your people to get out here NOW!"

"Okay, okay, okay," shot back Captain Singh. "People coming. Okay, okay, okay."

Then the return to more waiting.

When discussing heralded Alaskan chopper pilots, one would be well-directed to look up the veteran rescue swimmer Wil Milam, now retired and living in Soldotna. Milam, who would have given anything to have flown on the *Selendang Ayu* rescue, recalls that sometimes, while shooting the bull during the long day's work they often put in at the rescue swimmers' shop on the base back in Kodiak, he would pipe up and put the matter before his mission-ready compatriots.

"Okay, guys," he'd say. "If you were going to get caught out on a big-dark-stormy, which two pilots would you want up front?"

Every time, without fail, the vote and consensus would choose Russ Zullick and Robin Starrett. "I'm here to tell you," adds Milam, "that God created Russ Zullick to fly a helicopter." Zullick had only recently retired from the Coast Guard, and was flying copters for the Maryland State Police. In 2008, Robin Starrett lost his life in a plane crash on Kodiak Island when the cargo bay of the commercial airliner he was piloting suddenly opened.

Others might not have been the best sticks, but the good ones were smart enough to know they weren't. "You always wanted to be with them," says Milam, "because they knew their limitations," flew accordingly, and treated their crews with fairness and civility.

Then there was Gene Rush. The boys who rode with him often referred to him as "Sugar Rush," which is ironic, because the guy had the calmest demeanor. "I was in Dutch Harbor once," says Milam, "working on a DC-3

[case] that had crashed into the side of the mountain not far from there. It took us three days to get near the site, waiting on the weather. So, finally, just in case someone's still alive, we decide to fly up there and go for it anyway.

"On the way up you could see this williwaw coming down the mountain, and I'm like, 'Hey, you've got some snow blowing down on us.' And Gene looks up, and you could just see it coming—it's just this white wall of fury! We've got the right-side cabin door open, and it hits us, and all our ears pop, and we start to descend. We start diving down toward the water of some bay on our left."

The tension inside the helicopter started to rise, like the space shuttle soaring into the heavens. These gut-wrenching, molar-grinding, unspoken screams of cerebral fear seemed to say, "Ohhhh dear God, we've got water on our left! We got water coming up on our left! It's coming up fast! It's coming up fast! Here it comes! *OHJEEEZZZZUUSSSHHHH-CCCCHRIST! THIS IS IT!*"

And then the comforting sound of Gene Rush's reassuring, low-key voice resonated over their headsets. In a pleasant, crackling tone filled with this impossibly unruffled, down-home calm, he confidently, almost nonchalantly, walked those under his care through the mounting crisis.

"*IIIIIIII* got her!" he said, in the rising tone of some redneck beer ad. "Weeeee're good!" And they were.

And though it has little to do with this story, according to Wil Milam, "It was the third time the same couple, a guy and a woman, had been piloting a DC-3 together when it crashed in Alaska. This time, on the trip that killed them, they were hauling two thousand pounds of cod sperm."

Now, finally, as more of the *Selendang Ayu*'s crew started to make their appearance, the hoisting began in earnest. Throughout it, Dave Neel watched vigilantly out the left side of the cockpit as endless lines of storm waves rolled their way.

"All right, Doug," Neel announced. "Here comes a new set of waves. So let's back off and wait for them to pass."

Occasionally, rogue waves thirty-five and even forty feet high, with wave troughs stretching for several hundred feet from crest to crest, would come powering onto the scene, and the bow of the *Selendang Ayu* would range high, and dip low. But then the sea would sometimes go into a brief quiescent period, in which things would settle out, and Neel would say, "Okay, Doug. You're clear." And once more, Doug Watson would slip back in and begin flying in his precise parallel formation over the bow, and Brian Lickfield would respond by sending the basket down.

Though repeatedly staggered by the invisible fists of

wind, the moment a survivor rose from the freighter's deck, Watson would slide out and away from the vessel, and allow Lickfield time to bring the man up and pull him inside.

"Dave and I were working along together pretty good as a team," recalls Watson. "He was calling them out. He would tell me when to back off. I was just trying to focus on what I was doing on the deck, and this served to lighten the workload. That [hoisting] is much easier to do from thirty feet off the deck than, say, one hundred feet; it's much easier to do when you're hovering down low because you can see the buoyant motion of the bow and deck a lot better."

While some of the crew members making their way toward the hoisting area were Filipino, most were from India. Dave Neel was surprised that none of them were wearing anything more than ordinary street clothes under bulky, old-school life jackets. One deckhand staggering along the deck, trying to brace himself against the wind, wore a beehive-shaped turban on his head. He appeared to be attempting to signal something indecipherable with his hands to those in the H-60 hovering above.

A single hoist can take as little as two minutes to perform. Nine lifts, eighteen minutes. Neel's crew waited for nearly two hours to hoist the first crewman, and another hour to gather up the stragglers who made up that first load. What should have taken a few minutes had consumed nearly three hours.

At the time, Lt. Doug Cameron was flying the other H-60 "back behind us," says Neel, "three or four hundred yards away in a sort of overwatch position." He, too, was burning up his precious fuel as he waited his turn to hoist.

Now Neel radioed Cameron. "Hey, Doug! I don't think this is too smart, really, in this weather and with these seas, to take these folks over to the *Alex Haley*. Why don't I just run them back into Dutch. The way those guys just come trickling out on deck like they do, it's going to take you at least another hour to load up the next nine, and by the time you get yours, I'll be back and get the rest and we'll be done."

"No. We have to take them over to the *Alex Haley*," replied Cameron. "Those are our orders."

"I don't think so, man," replied Neel.

"David, take them over there."

Dave Neel's reluctance was understandable. The risks that came into play while trying to unload nine survivors onto the teetering back deck of a Coast Guard cutter on such a day were manifold. The seas were so high that often, as the *Alex Haley* crowned over the crest of a wave, her propellers would cavitate, spinning in midair, and when she sailed down into the wave trough beyond, her bow was forever "busting sea."

While Neel and Watson air-taxied their predetermined load of nine survivors over the *Alex Haley*, Doug Cameron and Pat Bacher began the hoisting. Maneuvering almost parallel to the ship's heading, on nearly the same course, they planned to slide sideways to the right to perform a particular hoist, and left to disengage from one.

It was obvious, however, that these guys never thought they'd end up in a situation like the one they now faced. One crewman wore only sweatpants. In between waves, another crewman took his camera out and began taking photos. Once again, when they lowered the rescue basket, several of the sailors down on deck began filling it with suitcases, duffel bags, and other personal belongings.

Running short on the kind of forced patience those who preceded him had shown, Cameron hailed the captain of the *Selendang Ayu* to try and make it clear exactly what was expected of him and his crew.

"Sir," Cameron explained, "a person must get into the basket every time. If they want to bring along a suitcase, too, that is fine, so long as it will fit into the basket along with him. But one person needs to get into that basket every time it touches down on your deck."

■   ■   ■

Then Dave Neel made a request to Cdr. Bell aboard the *Alex Haley,* asking permission to approach the cutter and offload the nine survivors that they carried. The request was granted. Neel and Watson planned to drop them off, lowering them one sailor at a time down onto the *Alex Haley*'s flight deck. But when he approached and saw how she was riding, his eyes went wide. The back deck of the cutter was heaving violently. Their plan looked far more perilous, now, than anyone had imagined.

When Dave Neel saw the pounding the cutter was taking, he thought "Oh, boy, this is really going to suck big-time!"

Watson's first order of business was to have Brian Lickfield pass a trail line down to the *Alex Haley*. Tied to one corner of the basket, they could use that rope line to guide each survivor down onto the rolling face of the cutter's flight deck.

So, when Watson swung in over the *Alex Haley* and spotted several members of her flight crew standing outside at the ready, he felt much better about attempting the kind of acrobatic flying he knew this part of the mission would entail. There were no better helpers anywhere to tend a trail line under such conditions than a fellow flight-crew member, because they knew how to do it perfectly.

As Watson approached, Lickfield tossed a coil of trail

line out the side door to the men below. For a time, as he worked to hover in place, Watson could look straight down on the flight deck. But as the ship bucked over each new wave, he soon became hopelessly out of rhythm, dangerously out of step with the heave and roll of the 283-foot vessel. Several times, the flight deck "came up, when we were going down." Were he to touch so much as an inch of one of his aircraft's rotor blades on the deck or superstructure of the cutter, people would likely die.

Then Watson's eyes focused on the wheelhouse of the *Alex Haley,* about two hundred feet ahead of him, and fifty or so feet back from the bow. He thought to himself, "If I can remain here and fly along in formation with the movement of that bridgeway, by the time my helicopter reacts, the approaching wave should just be getting here, and I won't be out of phase anymore." The more he thought about it, the more sense it made. He smiled inwardly. "I just might be able to make this happen."

Responding to the urgency of the moment, Doug Watson had plucked this clever new technique out of thin air. It would require total concentration, and a feathery touch on the jog-stick control to fly with such precision, but now, one by one, the human deliveries could begin. With Watson in close pursuit, the deck of the *Alex Haley* swept up over the waves, rising and falling as much as forty feet in a single cycle. (There is a video taken of him flying along, working to maintain station, mimicking the movements of the cutter's stern as it descended into the trough on that wind-flogged afternoon. The imposing dimensions of the steep, mountainous terrain of Unalaska Island rising and falling in the distance, bring the dizzying interactions between the ship, the helicopter, the backdrop, and the sea itself into a close visual perspective.)

Co-pilot Dave Neel soon found himself caught up in a remarkable ride-along, as Doug Watson performed "the fanciest bit of life-and-death flying that you have ever seen in your life."

The rear cabin of the H-60 was well along in emptying its human cargo, when Neel looked over at Watson.

"Doug, how are you doing this?" he asked.

Immersed in his groove and rhythm, Watson gave no reply.

One by one, the survivors landed on the teetering surface of the deck below. Somehow, Watson managed to keep in perfect sync with it, delivering each without injury, in a stylish, even eloquent demonstration of flying skills that those on deck would later describe as "absolutely amazing."

By focusing on the *Alex Haley*'s bridge mounted up forward, and using that as a reference point, Watson was able to make the necessary in-flight adjustments in time to allow him to, in effect, fly along in unison with the deck. So by the time the approaching wave actually reached the hoisting area directly beneath him, he was "already there."

Dave Neel glanced at Doug Watson, with his eyes fixed in the distance, and his two hands glued to the jog stick extending up from the floor between his knees.

"Doug," he said good-naturedly, "you look like a monkey fucking a football!"

Without altering his laserlike focus, Watson replied, "Well, I kind of *feel* like a monkey fucking a football."

"The conditions were pretty intense," recalls flight mech Brian Lickfield, "with seas up to thirty-five feet high lifting and tossing the ship about. We swung in over the back deck of the *Alex Haley*, and Doug Watson just started putting them down. That guy is an awesome pilot! He got into his own little routine, and he followed the ship over the tops of the waves and down into the wave troughs. You could see the land rising up and down in the background. He did some amazing flying that day, in absolutely the worst flying conditions in my fourteen-year Coast Guard career. He made my job so easy. I mean, I lowered those nine guys in no time. We got in sync and it was a continuous flow type of thing, like 'Bam! Bam! Bam!' "

One by one, flight mech Brian Lickfield lowered the grateful survivors down onto the cutter. And as the stern rose and fell as much as fifty feet in violent, unending cycles, Watson's flying was so precise that the sixteen-thousand-pound Jayhawk helicopter he was piloting remained locked in position over the flight deck, hovering there "like a statue."

With their last survivor safely on board the *Alex Haley,* Doug Watson sprinted back toward the *Selendang Ayu* thinking, "Okay. Now we're just gonna go pick up the final eight survivors and fly on home with them."

While enroute, however, they overheard a radio communication between Captain Singh and Cdr. Bell. The captain was claiming that his second—and last—anchor was now holding, that he was good to go, and that he was going to keep the other seven crewmen, who were mainly engineers, with him on board to try to finally get their main engine started.

"But, sir!" shot back the voice broadcasting from the *Alex Haley.* "We don't show your anchor holding. Our radar shows that you are sliding closer and closer to the shore!"

At about that time, Dave Neel was studying his fuel gauges and mentally calculating the air-time remaining before they reached "bingo," the absolute limit of time they had left to remain on scene and still reach the airport in Dutch Harbor without running out of fuel and dropping out of the sky.

"So what the hell am I supposed to do?" Neel asked himself. "Just hang around out here? We don't have enough fuel to do that!" Neel decided to call Doug Cameron, the commanding officer aboard the other H-60. He and Pat Bacher and their crew were just finishing up hoisting the second batch of nine sailors off the gyrating bow of the *Selendang Ayu*.

"Look, Doug," Neel told him. "You've got a full hour's worth more gas than we do. Somebody's got to remain out here on scene, and we're getting close to bingo. So why don't we land somewhere so you can transfer your survivors over to us. We'll take them back to Dutch Harbor while you guys remain on scene here and use your extra hour of fuel to hoist off the last eight, and then we'll be done with it."

Doug Cameron readily agreed.

Flying through the battering gusts to nearby Unalaska Island, they traveled down the coastline for several miles, located a more or less level patch of snow-covered ground inland, and landed the two aircraft. Then they quickly set about to transfer the nine survivors. With several hours of flying time under his belt since the last pit stop, Dave Neel climbed out of the H-60's cockpit to relieve himself.

Standing with his feet shoulder width apart, it was difficult enough, in all the noise and downdraft coming from the rotor blades spinning overhead, to maneuver himself into a proper firing position. But things had just started to flow when his "buddies" who'd been circling in a C-130 overhead, chanced to make a low pass at that moment, directly over him.

Complaining under his breath at the chances of experiencing such a complete invasion of privacy at such a remote time and place, Neel completed his business. Then, zipping up, he climbed back into the H-60 cockpit.

With another gratifying load of survivors safely on board, Neel and Watson lifted off and headed toward Dutch Harbor, leaving Doug Cameron and his crew on scene to complete the rescue mission.

The flight back to the airport near that famous fishing port was arduous. While enroute, something occurred that would significantly alter the course of events. Many would later look back on it as nothing short of providential. As they flew at approximately three hundred feet above the ocean, moving around the backside of the mountain range that stretches the length of Unalaska Island, Neel and Watson suddenly lost all radio contact with the outside world.

There is a Civil Twilight law at the Dutch Harbor Airport that bans all flying after dark. Although SAR mission flights are launched if at all possible, there are no scheduled flights in or out of Dutch Harbor after the sun sets. Neel and Watson could easily see why, now. As they maneuvered in for a landing, they were barely able to see the hangar through the veil of wind-whipped snow and closing darkness, though it was only thirty yards away. They taxied in, turned the nine survivors over to the local INS (Immigration and Naturalization Service) agents, and hurried inside for a hot cup of coffee.

True to form, back on scene Captain Singh was again refusing to release the last of his crew. Virtually powerless to alter that decision, and with Pat Bacher at his side, Doug Cameron began searching for a place to land on nearby Unalaska Island where "we could just sit . . . and wait . . . and conserve our fuel just in case." They soon came upon one such perch that they could "nestle" themselves into, but the mountainous terrain surrounding it was so "straight up-and-down," that they immediately lost all radio contact upon entering it. Their only option, they soon realized, was to just keep flying, and they were once again relegated to orbiting the freighter.

Earlier in the day, Lt. Cameron had talked with Cdr. Phillips, the operations officer back in Kodiak, and Phillips had told him that he wanted Cameron to be sure, at the end of the day, to end his mission by bringing CG 6021 back to Cold Bay, where a fresh new flight crew would be waiting. Cameron had set his "bingo fuel" for leaving the scene based on that scenerio. When, along toward dark, that moment finally arrived, he was forced to depart.

During their return trip to Cold Bay, Cameron and his

crew got "rocked around pretty good" by the air turbulence. The seas were huge. Then, fifty-eight miles from
their destination, an all-critical chip light flashed on, signaling a potential problem with the main gear box. "Our
two engines feed into the gear box above us," explains
Cameron. "They turn a set of big, heavy gears which make
the rotors turn, a lot of torque being applied." Their
concern was real. Should those gears come apart, their
helicopter would plunge into the sea like a dropped rock.

"There are five little magnetic chip detectors," says
Cameron. "In the event that the gear box starts to grind
and make metal chips, they will lodge in this little chip
detector. Then a light comes on in our panel telling us
that our main gearbox is starting to make metal, which is
definitely not good news."

The aircraft's chip light came on, and then went off.
Then it came on a little longer, and then went off. Then it
came on and remained on longer still, before finally blinking out again. Eventually, it came on, and remained on,
which was a reliable indication that "things were getting
worse up there."

And just that quickly, and due to no fault of their own,
pilots Doug Cameron and Pat Bacher found themselves
drawn into an increasingly tenuous situation. The unde-
niable facts were this: Caught in a tremendous blow, they
were flying alone at night over open water, in December
in freezing temperatures, with no ship or plane to provide

cover. Low on fuel, with their collective trim broken, huge seas powering past below, and the Aleutian Mountains crowding right down to the water's edge, wind-cell blasts of seventy and eighty mph repeatedly staggered them. And now, with the warning pulse of a panel chip light ratcheting up the stress level, the two pilots pressed on.

"Flying with our hearts in our throats," recalls Doug Cameron, "We finally touch down in Cold Bay. We land. We get out. And Chief Brian Daugherty, the senior maintenance person in charge, hops in, pulls the chip detector out, and finds a big, huge chunk of metal in there."

Daugherty turned to Cameron. "This gear box has got to be changed," he said matter-of-factly. "There's no way this aircraft is flying again until that has been completed!"

"So that is that," thought Cameron. For he knew it would require several days of heavy maintenance to replace the main gear box—including the use of cranes—before the 6021 could be repaired and returned to flight status.

Using the airport phone in Dutch Harbor, Dave Neel called the base in Kodiak to report in. It should be duly noted here, however, that a major glitch in their orders occurred. Apparently, there had been a breakdown in communications somewhere between Juneau, Kodiak, and Dutch Harbor.

"Hey," Dave Neel told the officer on duty at the time. "We have off-loaded the original nine crewmen onto the back deck of the *Alex Haley*. And now we've just finished delivering the second load of nine survivors back here in Dutch Harbor. We're getting fueled up now and plan to head back out to the scene to get the eight remaining crewmen off the *Selendang Ayu* as soon as possible."

"No, you guys are done," said the officer on the line. "The ship's captain is going to keep the seven remaining crewmen on board the freighter. Apparently he has an anchor in the water and thinks it's still holding. So you guys are clear to stand down for now. Top off your gas, and make sure your chopper is ready. You're going to be on stand-by tonight. Go grab a room at the Grand Aleutian [Hotel] there, and have yourself one of those seafood buffets."

Neel assured the officer that he and his crew were, indeed, looking forward to the soft, warm comforts of food and rest at the Grand Aleutian. When Neel returned to the hangar to spread the good news, he found the survivors from India posing for pictures alongside his helicopter, the 6020, the one that had just brought them back alive.

Unbeknownst to either Dave Neel or Doug Watson, since all communications with the *Alex Haley* were still blacked out, the *Selendang Ayu*'s anchor had continued to drag and was, at that moment, being driven up on the rocks in Skan Bay. It was clear to Cdr. Matt Bell, in the wheelhouse of the cutter, that neither they nor the tugboats still standing by on scene would be towing the *Selendang Ayu* anywhere on this day.

With her stern hard aground, and the wind and sea swells pushing her farther sideways, she had become a stationary target, a sitting duck for the huge groundswells and ocean breakers now powering ashore. With seven crewmen and their captain still trapped onboard, and darkness fast approaching, Cdr. Bell once again radioed the captain. He insisted in this latest call that the freighter was in grave danger of rolling over, and pointed out that it would be much easier to hoist the crewmen during the daylight hours than at night. Thus, he was finally able to win Captain Singh over, having impressed upon him the need to release the last of his men, and even to join them himself out on deck.

H-65 Dolphin pilots Tim Eason and Rob Kornexl were seated downstairs in the ward room of the *Alex Haley*, busily trying to work out the details of their hypothetical mission when the ops boss of the *Alex Haley* came running up.

"Well, the shit's really hit the fan!" he announced. "One H-60 is now broken down in Cold Bay. And we've lost all communications with the second 60 somewhere near Dutch Harbor, which means that we don't know *where* he is for certain. And of course now that both of our rescue choppers are no longer available, the skipper of the *Selendang Ayu* just called on the radio, saying that he's run aground, is taking on water, and is done playing around with his engine. And guess what? He says he wants to get off the boat, now."

Finally, turning to Eason, he asked, "Can you launch?"

Eason knew that they were "way out of limits." In fact, the pitch-and-roll limits for launching a chopper from the flight deck of a CG cutter while under way at sea was just five degrees of front-to-back pitch and seven degrees of side-to-side roll. Going strictly by the book, once they exceeded those limits they couldn't do anything. But Eason also knew of a code that ran deeper than rules. It went something like "the probability of saving a life warrants maximum effort." He glanced at his co-pilot Rob Kornexl. He'd relish the chance. The guy was born game.

"Okay," replied Eason. "Yeah, we can launch, if it has truly hit the fan."

The ops boss disappeared up the stairway. Eason and Kornexl looked at one another as if to ask, *In this weather? Is he really serious!*

Like any good flight deck captain aboard a CG cutter on Alaska's high seas, Dale Estilette and his crew had the

H-65 stored out of harm's way. Chained down as it was inside the hangar—which sits seventy-five feet or so from the center of the landing pad, on the aft-most portion of the stern of the *Alex Haley*—it "wasn't going anywhere." The hangar roof covering it is a retractable, three-piece partition standing twenty-five feet high, designed to slide back inside itself.

But the *Alex Haley*'s flight deck was presently being raked by fifty- and sixty-knot (60 to 70 mph) gusts of wind and sea spray, with waves 30 feet high and better carrying green water over her bow. The violent winter storm was strong enough to knock down a grown man and sweep the deck clean of him. No one dared to venture forth. Besides, with Dave Neel's H-60 due to return soon, the chances of being called upon to launch the ship's H-65 seemed nonexistent.

Those on board the *Alex Haley* tried repeatedly to contact Dave Neel's chopper. With a trillion-dollar communication system at their beckon, they could normally call anywhere in the world. "But we can't talk to someone twenty miles away," says Estilette, "when there's a six-thousand-foot-high mountain like the Makushin volcano in the middle."

And so with the freighter now hard aground, and no other helicopters available, H-65 pilots Tim Eason and Rob Kornexl joined Cdr. Bell and hiked back to the flight deck's av-shack (aviation shack) to have a little pow-wow with Dale Estilette. Once inside, they didn't mince words, putting it to Estilette directly. "How" they wanted to know, "do you feel about taking the H-65 out of the hangar and preparing it to fly?"

Given the fanatical penchant for safety on board Coast Guard cutters in Alaska, the idea of rolling the eight thousand-pound chopper out on the open deck and preparing it to fly in such weather seemed fairly ludicrous. Estilette's initial reaction was one of laughter.

"There's no way!" he exclaimed, amazed that they'd even consider it. "In these seas, we're so far out of limits, its incredible. Five and seven [degrees] are our limits. And right now we're probably looking at twenty and thirty!"

Cdr. Bell leaned close and made his flight captain a straight proposition.

"What if I can get you close to limits?" he asked.

"How many people are left on board this ship?" Estilette inquired.

"Eight."

Dale Estilette was further informed that Doug Cameron's H-60 had experienced a serious mechanical malfunction, and that Dave Neel's 60 had gone missing, vanishing into a communications blackout, or perhaps even lost in a collision with a mountainside—like those poor, unlucky souls who were flying in the fog off Kodiak Island did back in 1985, when they plowed into the top of *Ugak* Island.

There was no way to know what had happened to Neel and Watson and their vanished H-60 or sure, but there were multiple survivors still onboard the *Selendang Ayu* pleading to be rescued, and so Estilette was forced to revisit the unthinkable.

The *Selendang Ayu* was "already on the rocks," Eason told him. "They're ready to get off right now."

Estilette turned to Cdr. Bell.

"Look," he said, "if you can get me within limits, we can haul the plane out on deck, and then we can come back here and revisit the issue of actually taking off."

"Then get the plane ready," said Eason. "We're going to give it an attempt."

"Yes, sir," Estilette replied.

Cdr. Bell seemed pleased. Heading back toward the bridge, he strode out of the room.

Secretly, however, Estilette felt that they may have just "bitten off more than we could chew."

Seconds later, an announcement sounded over the ship's loudspeaker system: "Now all tie-down crew personnel report to the flight deck for helo roll-out!"

"Well, there's our answer," said Eason, as he and Kornexl began their preflight preparations.

FIVE

At the airport in Dutch Harbor, it took approximately forty-five minutes for Dave Neel, Doug Watson, Brian Lickfield, and Aaron Bean to refuel their H-60 helicopter #6020, move it to the other side of the runway next to the hangar, and get it squared away for the night. Dave Neel was walking over to the office to fill out the paperwork necessary to close out the mission, and the rest of the crew were sitting in a borrowed pickup truck—awaiting his return and looking forward to the welcome ride into town— when a Coast Guard vehicle screeched to a halt nearby, and a young Coastie called out to them.

"Hey, Lt. Neel! You need to call your Ops Center immediately! They want you on the phone right now!"

Dave Neel ran to the office and made the call. Bob Phillips, his commanding officer on the ground back at Air Station Kodiak, answered.

"Dave! Where are you?"

"I'm sitting here in Dutch Harbor," replied Neel, "filling out my paperwork."

"Why aren't you back out on scene?"

"Well, I didn't know I was supposed to be."

"What are you talking about? You guys are supposed to get gas and go right back out there!"

"Wait a second, Commander. I was told that we were to stand down."

"Look, Dave, you've got to get back out there. The 6021 has had mechanical problems and has been released from its on-scene duties. It's sitting broken in the hangar in Cold Bay, waiting to be repaired. The freighter has run aground, and its captain is now pleading to be taken off of her. We need you guys out on the scene immediately! Are you bagged?"

"No," shot back Neel. "We've got only four-point-eight hours on us. We still have enough flying time left. We can go."

"Are you tired?"

"We're not that tired! We'll go back out. Our tail rotor needs to be retorqued [tightened down]."

"Well, are you comfortable flying with it?"

"Yeah, no problem. It's not a big deal. I'm comfortable with that."

Neel heard a pause, as if his commander back in Kodiak was taking in new information from someone else speaking to him close by. Suddenly the officer's voice came back on the phone.

"Well, then, you gotta go!" he said. "GO! GO! GO!"

"Roger that," Neel shot back. Hanging up the phone, he sprinted across the tarmac to his men.

"All right, guys," he announced. "We gotta go back out."

The stunned looks on their faces said it all. Neel allowed them a moment to process the news, gather themselves, and mentally edge back into the game.

"Is everybody comfortable with that?" he queried. "The 6021 has had mechanical problems and is sitting on the ground in Cold Bay, broken and waiting for repairs. The *Selendang Ayu* has finally run aground. We're going to go out and get the last eight folks and bring them back, and then we'll be done."

So pilots Dave Neel and Doug Watson, flight mechanic Brian Lickfield, and rescue swimmer Aaron Bean once again hopped aboard the aircraft and set out to do the whole thing all over again. They made another low-visibility trip out of town, through the pass, and around the mountains. It grew dark. The transit was brutal; the journey, and the tasks awaiting them, daunting. And traveling in another total communications blackout, they had no way of knowing what was happening on scene.

All day, Cdr. Matt Bell and his staff in the wheelhouse of the *Alex Haley* had navigated through a blinding series of snow squalls. One minute, they could see for several miles in the distance, with the *Selendang Ayu* and the soaring mountain landscape of Unalaska Island showing clearly on the horizon. And then, the next snow squall would roll in and erase that vision, leaving them adrift inside a claustrophobic void of silver and white.

With darkness closing, the *Alex Haley* moved steadily ahead, her bow slicing through the tall, oncoming waves. Then, Rob Kornexl radioed the bridge asking Cdr. Bell if he would do a 180-degree turn, and begin running with the seas. This the skipper did in the hopes of providing a smoother ride and, hopefully, some of those durations of calm the flight deck crew would need to haul the H-65 out. Moving it into place in the middle of the flight deck, they would unfold her rotor blades and lock them in place, and get her prepped to fly.

Once Cdr. Bell had completed his turn, Estilette slid back the hangar cover. Now the work could begin. Normally, when the *Alex Haley* was under way, it took six or seven people to push the H-65 out from under the hanger and keep her steady. In the midst of such an unpredictable evening, however, approximately twenty joined in. Their efforts were greeted by another intense flurry of blizzard snow.

The launching pad is a rectangular-shaped platform of flat steel that stands approximately twenty feet above the water, and covers every inch of the *Alex Haley*'s stern. It is surrounded by a five-foot-high border, a steel-framed fence with netting stretched across it. Folded down flat, it provides a border of netting that extends, on three sides, well beyond the edge of the actual landing area. It is designed to catch anyone who might chance to stumble that way.

Measuring thirty-seven feet at its aft-most edge, the deck broadens slightly, and stretches toward the plane hangar constructed on the backside of the ship's superstructure. When not in flight, the H-65 is stored there, out of the weather and secured for running.

In the middle of the deck near the stern is a circular, steel honey-combed grid six feet in diameter. The talon probe is built into the belly of the H-65. It has twin beaks which, when triggered, extend straight down, sliding effortlessly into any number of prospective grid holes. Then they come together, drawing the helicopter down, attaching it to the ship. "It's a very comforting feeling, when the ship's under way," says Eason. Once that is engaged the H-65 cannot go anywhere, and can be considered secured. In fact, after the aircraft's talon is engaged, the *Alex Haley* could roll upside down and the helicopter would still remain locked in place. The problem on this night would be getting it there, traversing the pitching, spray-slickened deck in the inhospitable semidarkness.

Each of Dale Estilette's flight crewmen was dressed in a pair of coveralls, a helmet, a pair of gloves, and a life vest with flares attached. Some wore light parkas. Yelling to be heard above the wind, Estilette made every effort to make certain that his crew performed their duties in a safe manner, and to see that everyone emerged unscathed. Dispersing directions as he went, and using only manpower to move it, he and his crew began guiding the eight-thousand-pound copter along on its short, but precarious eighty-five-foot journey across the flight deck.

Several times, as he and his crew shoved the H-65 along, the ship began to leap and roll so brusquely that they halted their efforts and allowed the deck a bit of time to settle out, before pushing on again. For a time, Kornexl and Eason even pitched in, something pilots almost never do.

Once the H-65 Dolphin reached the landing pad, and her talon had been engaged, Estilette and his crew began the work of unfolding the chopper's rotor blades. Typically, Estilette used one man on top of the plane to insert the main rotor blade panel, and two others to walk each blade into place. On this primitive, elemental evening, however, he placed two men on top, and assigned four others to carry the blade and walk it into position. He insisted upon this because he knew that with the kind of winds they were encountering on the flight deck, sometimes the rotor blades "tried to take off on their own."

In good weather, unfolding the four rotor blades and locking them into position could be accomplished in as little as ten minutes. But with the boat pitching and rolling as she was, it took Estilette and his crew substantially longer.

One member of the flight deck crew didn't think they should be launching in such weather at all. Crewman Steve Schmid turned to Tim Eason and made his feelings known. "Sir, this is stupid. We shouldn't be doing this. The other helicopter is coming back. We know they're getting fuel. So what are we doing here? Why are we doing this?"

"Steve, the 6021 is gone," Eason explained. "And we don't really know *what* the 6020 is doing. So we have to launch." He paused. "Prepare to launch the helicopter."

Hearing the order removed any doubts as to whether or not they truly intended to attempt to fly the H-65 off the back deck. Without further comment, Schmid rejoined his crewmates.

Having received the order to prepare to launch, the flight deck crew members rushed to lower the individual sections into position. But, buffeted by the cold, ceaseless winds several of those sections refused to lie down and lock in place in their horizontal positions as designed.

"My net won't stay down!" announced one crewman. "It won't stay in place!"

"It's the wind!" yelled another. "The wind is blowing too goddamned hard! It's pushing them upright!"

As for the actual launching, Dale Estilette still felt quite dubious about it. Taking into consideration the merciless nature of the wind and seas, and the free-falling action of the *Alex Haley*'s bow, he thought, "There's no way that this launch is going to happen. We'll get somebody killed!" But soon after that he ran into Tim Eason and Rob Kornexl coming out of the preflight briefing room.

"Dale," said Eason, "all I want to know is thumbs-up, or thumbs-down? We'll do whatever you decide."

Estilette walked back out on deck to take another look at the weather. Darkness was closing fast. In the distance, he could see the freighter with her stern hard aground. In the glare of her deck lights, he could make out the storm waves exploding high and white against her midships. Now, more than ever, he was aware of the dangers the eight survivors still trapped aboard her were facing.

Estilette turned to Eason.

"Tell the captain to get us on the best possible launch path that he can find."

To take full advantage of the prevailing air currents, the H-65 must face directly into the wind during liftoff. With it anchored solidly in place on deck, Cdr. Bell once again reversed his course. Bringing the *Alex Haley* around 180 degrees, he pointed her bow directly into the wind, and began pounding straight into the oncoming seas. At that time, the ship took several more "really extreme pitches." Though it produced a far rougher ride, the increase in wind energy would provide Rob Kornexl and Tim Eason with the kind of additional lift their H-65 might need.

Moments later, Cdr. Bell called back to Estilette over the intercom and loudspeaker system.

"This is what you've got," he said. "This is our launch path right here."

Estilette turned to pilots Kornexl and Eason. "How do you boys feel?"

Both pilots assured him that they were up to the task.

"Can you lift off in this weather?" asked Estilette.

"Yes," said Kornexl, confidently.

"Yes, we can," added Eason, with equal assurance.

All eyes turned back to Dale Estilette. The flight deck crew boss wore a pensive expression on his face.

"Hey, we can do this, Dale," Kornexl assured him. "And we can do it safely. We'll get it done."

Estilette felt that "was a reasonable response." Eight lives remained in imminent peril.

"Well, then, I tell you what," replied Estilette. And holding out both fists, he gave them two thumbs-up.

Squinting against the cold and spray, Eason and Kornexl hurried across the pitching deck. The two pilots climbed into the cockpit of the waiting helicopter and strapped themselves in, while Greg Gibbons assumed his position as flight mech in the rear cabin. As agreed, Tim Eason took his place in the pilot's seat on the right, while Kornexl occupied the co-pilot's seat on the left.

Eason turned to Kornexl.

"Rob, you can have the takeoff," he said. "And once we get out to the wreck, I'll do the hoists."

Nearing the moment of liftoff, Estilette hustled his crew from the back deck. "Have a safe flight!" he called out as he passed the H-65. The prepping for takeoff had taken them just thirty-seven minutes to complete, a respectable time even during favorable weather on a cutter, but a phenomenal performance under such adverse conditions.

The flight deck crew gathered together inside the close, windowless aviation shack at the far end of the hangar. They would watch the H-65's liftoff there on their closed-circuit TV, and listen to the play-by-play of the building drama on their hand-held VHF radios.

"You are clear to start your engines," sounded the go-ahead communication from the wheelhouse.

Then the LSO (landing safety officer) gave the okay signal to the helicopter pilots to start the first engine. And the second. Next, he gave them clearance to release the rotor brake. The rotor blades started to turn. Finally, Tim Eason radioed Cdr. Bell in the wheelhouse, asking permission to take off.

"Preflight check list complete, sir," he said. "Request permission for a green deck."

"Absolutely," shot back Cdr. Bell. "Permission granted. Green deck."

"Tower. 6513. Request takeoff to port."

"Roger, 6513. You are clear to take off to port."

Once the pilots of the H-65 Dolphin helicopter received their go-ahead, they faced a trio of lights—red, yellow, and green—that were mounted in a vertical row, much like traffic signals. This one, however, was controlled from inside the wheelhouse.

Now, with the tall, ragged combers tossing the *Alex Haley*, and her flight deck constantly exceeding its maximum launch limits, Cdr. Bell nevertheless gave Eason and Kornexl the last official clearance, the unmistakable illumination of the green light, the final go-ahead, signaling that they were now clear for takeoff.

With the H-65's rotor blades fully engaged, and their speed and velocity steadily increasing, Rob Kornexl was preparing to lift off, when a tall, lumbering wave rolled out of the evening shadows and slammed into the *Alex Haley*. Staggered by the blow, the bow of the cutter rose sharply over the crest, and then plunged into the gaping canyon beyond.

The ship, the flight deck, and the chopper balanced upon it pitched forward a good twenty degrees nose-down. Had the talon not been holding the H-65 securely in its place, the copter would have almost certainly tumbled over, effectively crashing the aircraft without its ever having taken off.

With over three-thousand hours of in-flight time, as well as years of prior Army experience as a pilot flying joint "ship-helo opts" with the U.S. Navy, doing small-boat interdiction off naval frigates, and two ALPAT (Alaska Patrol) tours under his belt, Rob Kornexl felt fully confident in his abilities. One of his main concerns was that he not exceed the aircraft's torque limits during the takeoff. Along with that came the necessity of maintaining a level attitude and a clean break from the cutter.

Kornexl was sitting at the controls, his heart pounding. The rotor blades were spinning forcefully now, picking up more speed with each passing second, when he turned to Tim Eason and, speaking tongue in cheek, deliberately understated the obvious.

"Tim," he said, "I believe this is going to be a nonstandard takeoff."

Tim Eason turned to him and, without breaking a smile, replied, "No shit! Ya think?"

Kornexl harbored absolutely no doubts that he could perform a safe liftoff even under such exceptional conditions. But with his wife Kerrie, now seven months pregnant, awaiting his safe return back in Kodiak, he had everything riding on it.

For a time, as the whistle of the H-65 Dolphin's twin gas turbine engines rose, Kornexl sat and studied the seas in the hope of catching a stretch of calmer water between the mountainous sets now jostling them. As the sound of the engines climbed higher, Kornexl felt the deck rising and falling beneath him. And as the chopper's rotor blades spun wildly overhead, he began to chant silently to himself: "Ready. Ready. Ready. Ready." Then, as the deck began to rise, he felt a brief lull in the mounting tempest, and taking full advantage of it, he made his move, declaring secretly to himself, "GO!"

With the touch of a button, he released the talon. No longer attached to the ship, Rob Kornexl pulled pitch and took off. Going "full collective" then, he called upon a muscular dose of torque from both of the Bravo model's twin, 1,200-horsepower engines. Timing it perfectly with the rising deck, he felt the energizing force of the headwinds filling the helicopter's rotor blades, and the thrill of the robust, vertical lift driving him into his seat. The H-65 Dolphin seemed to almost leap off the deck, and dumping her nose to gain speed, Kornexl rocketed into the wind-ravaged skies. Aloft at last!

SIX

Still lost in a communications blackout, it was nearly dark when, just seconds before the H-65 lifted off from the *Alex Haley*, Dave Neel and Doug Watson flew out from behind the mountains of Unalaska Island.

Hurrying on through the jolting winds and the hazy islands of blizzard snow blowing past, they spied what they believed were the running lights of the two tugboats, and those of the *Alex Haley*, still standing by on-scene, laboring to hold their own positions.

Then Neel caught sight of the *Selendang Ayu* several miles in the distance. The sodium lights mounted atop her wheelhouse were rocking from side to side, filling the night with shifting beams of cold hard light. It was immediately apparent that her journey had finally come to an end. With her stern driven onto a reef, and her bow leaping high into the night, the shipwrecked *Selendang Ayu*, with her last remaining anchor still in tow, was lying almost side-to the oncoming waves. Shifting constantly she was, no doubt, punching any number of holes in her hull.

"Man, look at that!" Neel told Watson, as both men surveyed the sight. "Compared to where we left her, she's all the way up in there, now." He paused.

"Doug," he continued, "you'd better hail the *Alex Haley* and let them know we're nearly on-scene again before everybody freaks out. All right?"

Watson agreed. But when he tried to call the *Alex Haley*, nobody answered. As they drew closer, they began to pick up some odd-sounding radio communications coming from the cutter—things such as course headings, wind speeds, and the like.

Neel was puzzled. "Who are they talking to, anyway?"

The radio messages grew clearer. More distinct. They soon realized that it was Cdr. Bell in the wheelhouse of the *Alex Haley* talking with the pilots of the H-65. The aircraft was warming up on their flight deck. Her props were already turning. They were about to launch.

"What the hell are they doing?" said Watson.

Finally, it dawned on him. They were giving flight instructions to the pilots of their own H-65. Apparently, they were about to attempt to takeoff from the cutter's back deck.

Neel and Watson could hardly believe their ears. They'd lowered nine survivors down onto the leaping flight deck of the *Alex Haley* only a couple of hours before. And seeing how much worse the weather had gotten in their absence, flight mech Brian Lickfield thought that pilots Tim Eason and Rob Kornexl had to be absolutely crazy, in the menacing conditions, to be attempting such a stunt.

Neel turned to Doug Watson.

"Get ahold of them, Doug," he said, "and tell them not to launch the 65. There's no need to, now that we're here. They think there's no one on-scene to save these people."

Doug Watson tried repeatedly to contact them over his own powerful VHF radio, but strangely, once again, no one could hear him.

Once clear of the cutter's flight deck, Rob Kornexl flew the H-65 "straight toward the ship" several miles in the distance. As they closed on the grounded hulk of the *Selendang Ayu*, Tim Eason took over the controls of the helicopter. Drawing nearer, he was shocked by how vulnerable the oversized freighter appeared. He was aware that when a ship was under way at sea, driving forcefully ahead toward its destination, the swaying action of her hull and the slicing motion of her bow both served to dissipate much of nature's destructive force.

But, when a ship runs aground and gets lodged in place, as the *Selendang Ayu* had done, there is no longer anywhere for that energy to be released—except up. No ship could endure such a beating for long. Eason recalled seeing a Russian freighter once that had run aground on a reef off the coast of Puerto Rico. The vessel lay side-to oncoming breakers that were no more than ten feet high that day. Still, the walls of sea spray that erupted off the ship were monstrous.

With the *Selendang Ayu* stuck now, with her stern hard aground and seas three, and even four, times as high driving into her exposed side, she, too, had become a sitting duck. Weighing 1,500 pounds per cubic yard, these storm waves were impacting with almost unfathomable force along the full 738-foot length of her port side, producing tall and spectacular rooster tails of sea spray.

Tim Eason was closing fast on the *Selendang Ayu*, and was about to begin initiating the rescue plan, when he heard Doug Watson's voice hail them over the radio. H-60 chopper #6020 and its crew of four had apparently returned, and were doing just fine.

"Hey, Tim!" he began. "We just arrived back on scene. But I'm not really sure what you're going to be doing out here."

"Well," shot back Eason, "we didn't know where you

were. Or whether you were coming back or not. So we were going to pull these last eight guys off. We can take the first three, if you guys want to get the rest."

Watson agreed that such a plan was indeed plausible. "But," he added, "we can take everybody at one fell swoop like we've been doing all day. So, if you want us to take everybody, if you could just watch our back, we could do it all in one evolution."

Like any search and rescue pilot in Alaska, Kornexl and Eason didn't want to be left out of the game. They were, in fact, chomping at the bit to be of service, to play a useful part in the mission at hand. But now the mighty H-60, with its titanic power and carrying capacity, had returned. The 60 could do whatever the rescue required. It appeared that those talented flyboys off the *Alex Haley* were, once again, going to get aced out of the action, essentially relegated to the status of spectators. Rob Kornexl could sense the frustration rising in his crew. It weighed heavily on him as well.

Eason's first thought, as an aviator who'd been sitting on the *Alex Haley*'s bridge watching everybody else hoist survivors aboard their helicopters all day, was "Screw you guys! We were here first, and now we're going to hoist some people."

As someone who had flown hundreds of missions off Coast Guard cutters on patrol in the Bering Sea through the years, Dave Neel (inside the 6020) completely understood the crew of the H-65's desire to be a part of the rescue, as well as the pent-up emotions that their fellow pilots were feeling. Acknowledging on a gut level their recent escape from the confines of the *Alex Haley*, his measured response was delivered in a tone of empathy and respect.

"Well, now, you boys were on-scene here first," he said, acknowledging their efforts. "So what do you want to do?"

Eason's impulse was still to "get busy and do some hoisting." But he paused to think it through. The all-powerful H-60 Jayhawk could do whatever the rescue required. Promptly setting aside their personal desires and disappointment, Eason and Kornexl were able to make a quick, commonsense assessment of the situation.

Since the H-60 could easily carry all of the remaining survivors at once—or the weight of a Cadillac, for that matter, and fly off with it—intervening with their comparatively lightweight H-65 would only complicate the evacuation and push the time it took to hoist the men further into darkness. At such a high-test moment, they quickly concluded, intellect would triumph over emotion, and drawing upon a solid background of training and experience, the two quickly acquiesced.

"You know what," Eason began, "you guys have already hoisted nine people from this ship. You know the hoist. And you have the capability to pick up the last eight survivors and carry them in your cabin in one load. So go

ahead and execute the hoists. We'll just stand by and provide cover for you."

"Roger that," added Kornexl. "That makes a lot more
sense."

As the 6020 moved into position, Eason made one
"racetrack pattern" loop, flying along at an altitude of about
three hundred feet around the entire ship. For a time, on
the downwind part of that orbit, they encountered another
snow squall, and visibility dropped to nothing.

Facing into the wind in front of the cliffs, Eason and
Kornexl placed their aircraft in a high, hovering position
several hundred feet above and well behind Dave Neel.
They would remain there, watching over their brothers,
as the H-60 hoisted the last eight survivors off the sinking
freighter.

Dale Estilette knew full well that as pilots went, Rob
Kornexl and Tim Eason were both "great sticks." In
fact, through the years he'd flown with each on different
missions. Just minutes before, Estilette and his men had
witnessed their takeoff on the closed-circuit TV inside the
aviation shack room. The H-65 appeared to literally cata-
pult off the deck. It was an impressive performance, and
the crowd of sailors who had gathered there to watch it
cheered aloud.

Now, standing by inside the wheelhouse of the *Alex*

Haley, Estilette overheard the ongoing discussion between the pilots of the two helicopters. He could see the H-65 in the distance, remaining on-scene, trying to hover nearby in the contentious winds.

"The H-65 was in forward flight," he recalls. "But they weren't moving an inch, or going anywhere, because they were flying in a hurricane."

Dave Neel and Doug Watson had arrived on-scene to find that the *Selendang Ayu* had moved dramatically from where they had last seen her. As they drew nearer, now, in the closing darkness, they could see how the stern of the *Selendang Ayu* had come to an uneasy rest on the outside edge of the surf zone. Rocking heavily from side to side within the theater of her own light, the ship was taking a terrible beating.

Her starboard anchor chain swept down from the bow and disappeared into the water. The anchor was apparently still attached, but had slipped badly, leaving the entire port side of the freighter lying almost completely broadside to the oncoming seas. Repeated wave strikes sent vast new eruptions of sea spray flying.

The *Selendang Ayu*'s bow continued to soar into the night. Doug Watson swung in behind the stranded freighter, and made his approach on her port side, passing over the crashing white streamers of groundswells pounding ashore just off her stern.

Now, as they flew along parallel to the ship, they came upon the heartening vision of the last of the crewmen massed together near the original hoisting place, on the port side, just aft of the bow. Neel and Watson felt encouraged by the sight. It looked like they just might be in and out of there and back in Dutch Harbor in time for the seafood buffet. Heroes tossing back frosted mugs of cold beer.

Doug Watson ran quickly through the rescue checklist. That completed, he pushed ahead, trying to jockey in as close as possible in the erratic winds. Watson was understandably feeling confident. Earlier, as the deck rose and fell, he'd hoisted nine survivors from precisely the same position. Now he planned to repeat the performance. He would begin this hoisting effort from a hover of little more than thirty feet above the deck.

Watson maneuvered the helicopter into position, and hung there, oscillating in a tenuous hover, as invisible bursts of wind pelted him. He'd hardly begun, when the voice of flight mechanic Brian Lickfield resonated over the radio.

"Basket going down, sir," he said.

Lickfield sent the rescue basket out, and let it sail back on the wind. He maneuvered it down and landed the basket directly in front of the eight remaining crewmen, then waited eagerly for someone to climb in. But to his consternation, no one moved! The crewmen from India "just stood there and looked at it." Such behavior was confounding. And unnerving. Brian Lickfield was furious.

"What the hell?" he said aloud. "Sir," he added finally, "they're not getting into the basket! Nobody's getting in! They're not even moving toward it!"

For as long as the rescue basket sat on the deck, Watson made it his calling to remain "anchored" there in the air. Hanging it out there on the edge like that, in the midst of such blustery conditions, was challenging enough, but the lack of cooperation down on the deck seemed illogical. Unbelievable. And as Watson fought to maintain his hover, and Neel kept on alert for the approach of any new wave sets coming their way, Lickfield tried everything possible to draw the men toward the waiting basket.

Whatever the reasons for such bizarre inaction down on deck, Doug Watson needed to concentrate fully, in the flailing winds, to maintain a semblance of proper position. Although he was committed to remaining there he was also fully aware, as he worked the H-60's controls, that the ship had drifted into the "break zone," and that the storm waves were now riding the lumbering groundswells to new heights as they neared the coastline. Reacting to the submerged topography of the shallowing waters, they were summoning their forces for a final, headlong assault onto shore.

The seas were clearly larger than anything they'd seen so far. Having traveled unhindered across several hundred miles of open water, the waves stood up sharply now. As they neared the reef-laden shallows of Unalaska Island, the waves were transforming themselves into monstrous, groaning breakers that continued to rock the defenseless ship. Worse yet, since night had fallen, the waves moved like shadows out of the surrounding darkness. They would be considerably more difficult for Dave Neel to spot.

Their troubles with the listless crewmen on deck below, however, remained unchanged. "They are not moving sir," reiterated Brian Lickfield. "They are not getting in."

"Brian, abort the hoist," Doug Watson said disgustedly.

Lickfield reeled the basket back up and sat it in the wind-raked doorway. Watson slid the H-60 chopper out and away from the ship. Then he paused to regroup. Moments later, and with little comment, Watson swung back into position. Lickfield pushed the rescue basket out the door. Perched in the doorway of the rear cabin, with one hand on the hoist control and the other on the handle molded into the wall on his left, he peered intently down over the side and soon guided the basket to another successful landing very near to those on deck.

But again, to his astonishment, the group of shivering sailors ignored the basket and remained frozen in place. Huddled together with their arms wrapped around one another's backs, they refused to move. Lickfield was beside himself. Whenever one of the crewmen would glance up at him, he and Aaron Bean would motion frantically to him, imploring the sailor to climb into the rescue basket. But, once again, the survivors refused to move.

"Hello!" yelled Lickfield, doing his best to be heard over the deafening roar of the helicopter. The men did not budge.

"Let me help you!" he pleaded. "Get in the basket! Do something!"

"Enough of this B.S.!" said Lickfield.

He reeled the basket up and pulled it inside. Neel and Watson backed off then, to refigure their approach. As they peeled away, Lickfield took in the overall size of the ship below. The pivoting deck of the vessel stretched six hundred feet in front of him and ended abruptly at the base of the blocky, white form of her wheelhouse. Powerful decklights mounted in precise rows along the outermost edges of the roof of the wheelhouse continued to illuminate the hoisting area and the spectacular fountains of sea spray.

One after another, a staggering barrage of craggy waves came barreling over her hand railings and across the middle of the ship's deck. The brutish demonstrations of power were a constant reminder that anyone caught by such an unbridled force stood little chance of surviving.

Equally worrisome to the freighter's lightly clad, inappropriately dressed seamen, was the spectacular discharge of static electricity created by the aircraft's rotor blades.

Streaking down the hoist cable, these powerful charges leapt from the nearest corner of the stainless-steel basket and struck the wet steel surface of the deck like a bolt of blue lightning. Sometimes leaping through the night air for several yards, these miniature thunderbolts promised to deliver powerful, and exceedingly unpleasant, shocks to anyone in direct contact with the basket.

Several times, as Lickfield lowered the rescue basket, he caught the leaping flash of static electricity discharging into the deck at their feet.

"It was no wonder, then," he reasoned, "that those boys are frightened. But did they have to wander out on deck on such a brutal Alaskan night dressed like a bunch of frigging high school students?"

Slapped right and left by the pelting winds, Watson continued to fight to maintain a stable hover. He managed to remain in place for several minutes, but still no one stepped forward. Their complete lack of response looked as though it might just go on indefinitely.

"Well, then," said Dave Neel, his voice filled with disgust, "bring the damned basket back up."

"Basket's coming up," replied Brian Lickfield. "Basket's inside the cabin."

Doug Watson shuffled up and away from the *Selendang Ayu*.

"How about sending Aaron down?" suggested Lickfield.

"No," countered Dave Neel, without hesitation.

Lickfield didn't press it. Lt. Neel could think well on his feet. Regardless of rank, he was a pilot with a reputation for remaining open to reasonable discourse from all members of his crew.

At that moment, Dave Neel was, in fact, comtemplating lowering Aaron Bean down onto the deck. Once again, he recalled that similarily hellish, black and inhospitable night he'd flown on a mission over in Prince William Sound. A salmon tender and its two-man crew had lost its steering and were drifting in the dark through a murderous, breaking sea. Ordering both crewmen into their survival suits, and into the water, he used a technique known as "direct deployment," in which the rescue swimmer remains attached to the hoist cable, is lowered down and, clutching each man securely in his arms, hauls the survivors up, one at a time.

That wouldn't work on this night, however. The present circumstances and its requirements were different. After mulling the present situation over, Dave Neel soon concluded that Brian Lickfield's idea had some merit after all.

"Aaron," queried Neel, "how would you feel about

going down on deck there and getting this operation under way?"

The rescue swimmer did not hesitate.

"Yes, sir," he eagerly replied. "I'll go down."

"Okay, then, Aaron," added Neel. "Why don't you get
into that basket and go down there and start kicking
some of those folks in the ass! Go down there and get those
people in the basket! Help facilitate this. All right?"

"Yes, sir!" Aaron Bean replied enthusiastically.

As he had been trained, Bean grabbed his rescue swimmer's bag containing his state-of-the-art "high-speed" rescue swimmer's dry suit and essential cold-water gear
including a hood, mask, snorkel and fins, and began the
hurried process of donning the gear when Dave Neel in-
tervened.

"No, Bean," he said. "Just get in the basket."

Lickfield would remember exchanging few brief words
with Aaron Bean as he helped the young rescue swimmer
into the basket and prepared to lower him. But the inher-
ent nature of the task was already understood. "Let's just
get these guys, and haul ass!"

They wanted to place Bean down on deck to act as a
kind of "traffic controller," recalls Lickfield. It would be
his job to "sort the people out and get things going down
there." Wearing only his air crew coveralls, a light, anti-
exposure dry suit, and his helmet, Bean climbed quickly
into the basket, put his head down, and placed both of his

hands under his buttocks. Then Lickfield swung him out the door into cold space.

To Aaron Bean, the roar of the helicopter was deafening, the prop wash fierce, and he thought to himself, "Well, this is what I trained for. So here goes!"

As he descended toward them, the survivors were sitting, huddled together, frozen in place on some pipes that ran along the base of the cargo hold, just yards from the original hoisting area. Not one of them made an effort to assist Bean as he landed. Yet Lickfield lowered him onto the heaving surface of the deck without a hitch, setting him down only a few steps from the crewmen.

The instant the basket touched the lunging, wave-swept deck, Bean leapt to his feet and raised one hand above his head. With palm open and all fingers aligned, he signaled those overhead that he was okay. Then grabbing the rescue basket, he hiked briskly up the steep slope of the pitching deck to where the dripping sailors from India were gathered. Bean had to pick up his knees and lean into the body of the rocking vessel to make way. It was like scaling a mountain. He found them huddled together against the frigid elements in a kind of collective, ongoing act of denial.

Bean marched up to the nearest crewman, grabbed him by the top of the vest, and muscled him into position inside the rescue basket. Then he flashed a look at Brian Lickfield squatting in the doorway of the H-60 overhead, gave him the thumbs-up sign, and watched as both man and basket rocketed into the sky.

While Brian Lickfield reeled up the first survivor and the helicoper swung away, Bean joined those left behind. He sat down beside them on the twenty-inch-thick horizontal length of pipe they were perched upon, about twenty feet from the port-side hand railing, and held on. When he looked out across the water to see what they were looking at, he took in the unrestrained image of the first of a volley of storm waves marching straight toward them. From their vantage point, the shadowy silhouettes of the powerful ocean waves lumbering their way looked massive.

Then the giant freighter took a sharp roll to port, and he and the others suddenly found themselves looking directly into the face of a fast-moving, monstrously large storm wave. It was like being seated on an E-ticket carnival ride in which you were taken to the very edge of disaster, deliberately placed in harm's way, and forced to linger there. Then, at the bottom of its roll the giant, teetering ship seemed to stall on its side. The wave looked as though it was about to plow directly into them when, at the last second, the ship began to roll back to starboard, lifting those so assembled high into the air, just as the full force of the approaching comber slammed into the vessel's underside.

"Whoa!" thought Bean. "This is wild!"

Aaron Bean could appreciate now why they hadn't rushed to assist him, or felt free to help one another climb into the rescue basket. They were terrified, and immobilized by that fear. He hoped to ease some of those fears by walking in the trenches right along with them as they waited to be airlifted; by standing beside them and facing down the intimidating mountains of closing waves as often as they arrived. Frozen in place, the inadequately dressed crewmen from India had been just plain "scared shitless."

At the highest point of the sweeping roll, they looked to be a good fifty feet above the water. But when he got them to their feet and began herding them toward the hand railing, out of nowhere the entire group got pounded by a sneaker wave that broke up and over the side. The wall of ocean water took them by surprise, staggering, and nearly leveling, the entire congregation.

The comber struck Bean "like a punch in the chest," and sent him sprawling. Waist-deep seawater seeking escape began rushing around the eight-foot-high cargo holds. And as the deck rolled to starboard, and the slant of the deck grew steeper, the water began to spill into the nearest channel, between the cargo hold and the wall housing the fo'c'sle compartment.

The power of the rushing water carried Aaron Bean

down the deck for forty feet or more. Regaining his footing, he began double-timing it back up the sloping deck to the hoisting area and the stunned and dripping survivors waiting there. Breathing hard, freshly doused in ice water, he was reaching out to grab ahold of the rescue basket when he saw a thick, blue arc of static electricity leap from the nearest corner of the basket to the sea-slickened deck.

Thinking the buildup of static electricity had been safely discharged, Bean reached out and grabbed the basket, and "POW!" it sounded, shocking him all up his left arm. Bean let go immediately, for it was stronger than anything he'd ever experienced. Now, more than ever, he could understand why the crewmen had refused to come anywhere near the rescue basket.

Choosing to ignore the painful hazard, the gutsy young recruit grabbed the second survivor by the front of his life preserver, walked him across the deck to the rescue basket, and stuffed him inside. A moment later, he was sailing aloft.

Using hand signals and direct, hands-on contact with the shivering crowd of survivors, Aaron Bean did his best to communicate his intent. But he did not speak their language, and with the roar of the H-60 hovering so close and loud overhead, it was hard to hear one's own thoughts. Bean had tried to prepare for the noise. He'd lined his helmet with high-density sound-canceling insulation, and wore custom-made ear plugs as well. Still, the sound was harsh and penetrating.

Having had enough of the crew's passive behavior, Aaron Bean grabbed the next sailor, walked him over and crammed him into the waiting basket. Once more, he gave a quick thumbs-up sign to Brian Lickfield, crouched in the doorway of the aircraft overhead, and then stood back as he yarded another survivor into the air.

At times, the helicopter seemed so very near, but Bean knew full well that Doug Watson was a pilot who was not too timid to get up close and personal. Even in such erratic and forceful headwinds, when the ship would move up, he would move up, and when the ship would move down, he would move down. "Watson was, like, acrobatic," says Aaron Bean. "He was on top of it. He was awesome!"

SEVEN

Some of Aaron Bean's first encounters with the crewmen of the ship involved trying to communicate a sense of urgency, while exercising a degree of order and common sense on deck. When one crewman tried to load his suitcases into the rescue basket, instead of climbing inside himself, Bean protested.

"No!" he yelled. "No luggage! Just you!" He paused, adding, "Now when you get in the basket, sit on your hands! And when you reach the helicopter, do *not* try to get out! Just stay in the basket until they pull you inside the cabin and kick you out!"

The northwest winds were cold and unrelenting, and the huddle of crewmen awaiting their turn in the basket were nearly flattened by several huge waves. One of the survivors, who spoke some broken English, asked Aaron Bean what he and the others should do. Making the sign of the cross on his chest, Bean advised them to "just pray that you make it off the ship."

From the outset, Captain Singh had been running around, hugging his leather briefcase.

"Can I take my case?" he asked, hopefully.

To Bean, fully involved in his survival mode, the man's problem seemed irrelevent; his repeated questioning in regard to it, irritating.

Another crewman was trying to warn Bean about something apparently catastrophic that was about to happen. But because of the language barrier, and the deafening roar of the H-60 fighting to maintain position in a close hover overhead, he couldn't decipher so much as a syllable of the sailor's emotional delivery.

Next, several more of the deckhands approached him carrying their suitcases.

"No!" Bean shouted, angrily waving them off. "I said no luggage!"

Bean was so "amped up," to emphasize the point he seriously considered tossing their suitcases over the side. Instead, thinking better of it, he pointed to the next survivor sitting on the pipe, and motioned to him with his forefinger.

"You!" he shouted. "You're next! Come here!"

■   ■   ■

Dave Neel and Doug Watson, in the chopper overhead, were pleased to note that with Aaron Bean on deck things were finally beginning to happen. Several hoists were carried out in quick succession. Then Neel spotted a set of swells rolling toward them and gave warning. Watson slipped sideways in the wind, and waited for them to pass.

It was during their third hoisting cycle that "this huge wave" came crashing over the bow. Looking out the side door of the rear cabin, Brian Lickfield could see it all. There was real force behind it. The waist-deep seawater "knocked Aaron Bean on his ass," he says, and swept him down the rolling, tilting deck.

Pilots Neel and Watson were facing forward at the time, and were unable to view the mishap. So Lickfield radioed them with the news.

"Sir, Aaron just got washed down the deck," he said. "But he's okay."

Once again, as Lickfield watched, the moment Bean had regained his footing, he ran back, grabbed the next person in line, and escorted him over to the hoisting area. Doug Watson was sliding the H-60 back over the top of the deck when a burst of wind struck, rocking him out of position. The aircraft's tail rotor came to within an arm's length of striking the cross-shaped foremast on the bow.

"Move left," Lickfield radioed Doug Watson over his headset. "Easy left."

Watson swung to the left, abandoning his hoisting position.

"So, what's up, Brian?" he wanted to know.

"Sir, you came really close to hitting the mast with the tail rudder," warned Lickfield, breathing much easier now. "You just can't get that close, sir."

"Well, what do you want to do?"

Lickfield answered for everybody. "Let's finish this. Let's just get it done."

Flying somewhat higher then, and moving slightly forward of where he had been, Watson maneuvered back into position. Hoists number four and five came off without a hitch.

Another tall wave broke over the bow and, once again, carried Bean down the sloping deck. His reaction? Same deal. He hopped up, shook it off and, between waves, ran back and immediately began muscling the next crewman into the rescue basket.

All parties were aligning themselves to hoist their sixth survivor when a snow squall blew in over them. Watson did not want to abandon the remaining survivors. But, illuminated in the radiant power of the mastlights, the visual effect of being accosted by countless, glowing crystals of swirling snow produced an almost instantaneous

Rolling heavily and about to run aground in the Aleutian Islands, the *Selendang Ayu* takes a beating as giant storm waves drive her ever closer to shore. *(Photo credit Dale Estilette)*

Cutting through the storm in Alaska's Bering Sea, the Coast Guard cutter *Alex Haley* plows through tail waves in pursuit of the drifting freighter. *(Photo credit Dale Estilette)*

TOP: Ready to hoist, an H-60 hovers over the bow of the *Selendang Ayu*. But the crew aboard the powerless freighter is doggedly slow at coming forward. At this point, the freighter's port side anchor is deployed but dragging badly. Notice the 120-foot seagoing tugboat *Sidney Foss* standing off. Trying valiantly to turn the freighter's bow into the wind, the tugboat was being towed backwards by the storm-tossed vessel, when the nine-inch towline they were using suddenly broke. *(Photo credit U.S. Coast Guard)*

LOWER LEFT: A mammoth wave strikes the midship area of the *Selendang Ayu*, as it drifts sideways through the building seas. *(Photo credit Dale Estilette)*

LOWER RIGHT: The errant freighter drifts toward the shore as an H-60 Jayhawk helicopter hovers high overhead. *(Photo credit Dale Estilette)*

THIS PAGE, LEFT: Buffeted by violent storm winds, Lt. Doug Watson tried to bring the H-60 Jayhawk helicopter into a hover over the *Alex Haley*'s pitching stern in order to lower nine survivors down onto her heaving flight deck. *(Photo credit Dale Estilette)*

RIGHT: Flying with remarkable precision, Doug Watson dances on the razor's edge between survival and disaster. Faced with a flight deck that soars and plunges as much as fifty feet in a single wave cycle, he creates an in-flight maneuver all his own. *(Photo credit Dale Estilette)*

BOTTOM: Zoom in of the same scene. *(Photo credit Dale Estilette)*

Just hours before the deadly crash, Lt. Watson fights to keep his 16,000-pound helicopter in position in the 50 knot (60 mph) winds. He is able to mimic, almost perfectly, the sweeping movements of the *Alex Haley*'s stern, as his crew lowers another survivor down onto the flight deck. *(Photo credit Tim Eason)*

The *Alex Haley* standing off several miles from shore. Notice the H-60 hovering in over her stern flight deck. *(Photo credit U.S. Coast Guard)*

The mighty *Selendang Ayu* rolls heavily in the building groundswells. Notice the sharp incline and cliff-lined shores of Unalaska Island. *(Photo credit Dale Estilette)*

The giant freighter continues to drag anchor. A Coast Guardsman aboard the *Alex Haley* leans on their deck cannon and studies the surreal sight, an environmental disaster in the making. The oil spill caused when the ship ran aground and broke up eventually coated some twenty-five miles of shoreline. The cleanup and salvage operation took eighteen months to complete at a cost of nearly $100 million. *(Photo credit Dale Estilette)*

H-65 Dolphin's flight mechanic Greg Gibbons studies the waves from the back deck of the *Alex Haley*. *(Photo credit Tim Eason)*

A disemboweled chunk of twisted metal and wire is about all that was left of the oil-covered, $16 million H-60 Jayhawk helicopter that crashed into the Bering Sea. Of the ten men aboard, six were killed on that violent December night. *(Photo credit Joe Metzler)*

Coast Guard rescue swimmer Joe Metzler stands beside the wreckage of the H-60 Jayhawk helicopter that was swept from the sky by a monster wave during a rescue attempt the night before. No trace of those who perished was ever found. *(Photo credit U.S. Coast Guard)*

Lt. Tim Eason, Flight Mechanic Greg Gibbons, and Lt. Rob Kornexl stand in front of the H-65 Dolphin they rode into the history books. The three heroes were awarded the Distinguished Flying Cross for saving six lives on that wild, wind-swept night. *(Photo credit U.S. Coast Guard)*

Survivors of the crashed H-60 helicopter crew, and those from the H-65 who saved them, share fellowship and beer—two weeks after their memorable mission—at a Christmas get-together at Dave and Rose Neel's home in Kodiak. Standing, from left to right: Lt. Tim Eason, AST3 Aaron Bean, Lt. Doug Watson, Lt. Dave Neel. Kneeling, from left to right: Lt. Rob Kornexl, AMT2 Brian Lickfield, and AMT3 Greg Gibbons. *(Photo credit Rose Neel)*

H-60 Coast Guard helicopter 6021, flown by Lt. Doug Cameron and Lt. Pat Bacher, shortly before mechanical problems forced them to retire to Cold Bay. *(Photo credit Dale Estilette)*

state of vertigo. With the ship, sea, and horizon all lost to him now, he was forced to abandon the hoist.

Doug Watson veered away, and accelerated into the sky. Concentrating entirely upon the altitude indicator—also known as the "artificial horizon," a horizontal, wing-shaped gauge on the face of the instrument panel before him—he worked diligently to keep the floating bar level. Flying along at fifty knots (60 mph) but remaining almost stationary in relation to the sea below, he needed to hang on long enough for the squall to pass. When the snow began to clear out and the whiteout surrounding them had faded to a light haze, Watson took in the comforting vision of the *Alex Haley* standing off and idling along, her running lights glittering in the distance.

As the squall continued to recede, Dave Neel felt there was little reason to wait.

"Look, guys," he announced, "I don't know how long this one is going to last. But the hoisting area still looks pretty good to me. Nothing has really changed for you guys in back. So how's about we just continue hoisting?"

Watson and Lickfield readily agreed.

Doug Watson moved back into place then, and he and his crew performed the sixth hoist. Lickfield pulled the survivor into the rear cabin, and readied for the next. Only one sailor plus the ship's captain remained. Then Aaron Bean would take his turn.

But trouble was building, both in the air and on the sea. The storm was clearly intensifying, and the wind gusts now arriving on scene began slamming into the copter, shaking the aircraft to its rivets.

As always, each time Neel would warn of the approach of a particularly large wave Watson would disengage from that hoist, bank lithely away, and accelerate into the sky. Occasionally, some of the wave strikes exploding off the freighter's side produced geysers of sea spray five and six stories high. A couple of times Watson even caught the patter of a few droplets across his windshield, but it was nothing to get in a twist over.

With the ship's sodium lights still illuminating the immediate area, Watson could see the deck below reasonably well out the lower portion of the right side of his cockpit window. By concentrating completely, he was able to reestablish both position and cadence in his efforts to mimic the movement of the vessel's foredeck.

Now, as he watched, a wave mushed over the peak of the *Selendang Ayu*'s soaring bow, flooding the deck area between the cargo hold and the fo'c'sle, and drenching Aaron Bean and the ship's captain, the last member of the ship's crew, in bone-chilling water.

Then, quite unexpectedly, Doug Watson began to experience a critical loss of reference. From the beginning he'd flown almost parallel to the alignment of the ship, with Lickfield trailing the basket back on the wind from just off the bow. For some reason, however, things seemed to be changing. Either the wind had shifted slightly, or the anchor was slipping again and the bow of the freighter was being carried farther into shore. As a result, his view of the bow, which had served as his only substantial reference, began to slip away and was soon lost altogether.

Regardless, Doug Watson maneuvered back into position, nose pointed into the wind, to hoist the seventh survivor. Lickfield trailed the rescue basket down at top speed. It was then that Dave Neel spotted a new set of waves rolling toward them. A thousand or so feet in the distance, he could make out only the dim outlines of them, at first. They were moving across the face of the sea, like wrinkles passing along the length of a settling blanket. As they drew closer, however, Neel thought they looked "significant. Particularly large."

Aaron Bean stuffed the seventh crewman into the rescue basket and, glancing overhead, had just given Brian Lickfield the thumbs-up when Dave Neel broke in over the intercom.

"Hey, guys," he said. "We've got a fairly large wave in this set coming in. I think this is a pretty good-sized one. We'll have time to pull off this hoist, but then we're going to need to move back and wait." He paused. "Doug," he added, "you're going to have to move back and left after this hoist. Wow, this *IS* a big one! You're really going to have to come up. You're going to have to come back and left and up. Back and left and up."

"Man coming up," reported Brian Lickfield in a steady tone.

Not once did Dave Neel's gaze leave the distant sea.

As the wave set moved out of the darkness and into the illuminating glare of the ship's floodlights, he was better able to scrutinize it. And he could see now that one of the waves closing on them was easily twice the height of the others.

"Holy shit!" announced Neel again. "Look at the *size* of that wave! This is a huge wave. A *huge* wave!"

Lickfield could sense the urgency in Neel's voice, and immediately began "two-blocking" the hoist, maxing it out, hauling up the present survivor as fast as the winch would bring him.

"Basket's clear, sir," Lickfield announced. "You can move left as far as you want now." He paused. "Man coming up."

"Now, *move!*" Neel ordered Watson, bringing the approaching threat front and center. "Back, left and up, Doug," he added in a steady tone. "Back, left and up."

Doug Watson moved back and left like he had all day, but he still wasn't coming up fast enough to satisfy Neel.

"All right, come up, Doug. Come up. Come *UP!*"

Watson moved back and left, rising steadily as he did so, but his rate of ascent was still not enough to satisfy his flight commander.

"You gotta come up!" added Neel, the tone of his voice jumping a full octave. "You gotta come up!"

Dave Neel grabbed the collective—the long, horizontal accelerator arm mounted alongside his seat—and, momentarily overriding Doug Watson, started "pulling power."

Doug Watson could feel Neel begin to pull on the collective arm, essentially gunning the aircraft's gas pedal. After so much success, and nothing short of masterful flying throughout the numerous hoisting evolutions he'd performed that day, he felt "a little testy" about having his judgment so suddenly overridden by his commander. Secretly, he suspected that Neel may have overexaggerated how high they really needed to go.

Flying into the stratosphere was a waste of time. Besides, such a maneuver would take him well out of his game, and with only Aaron Bean and Captain Singh left to hoist, he wanted desperately to get back into position and make the saves.

But Neel continued to pull unrelentingly on the collective. As the helicopter accelerated into the sky, Watson again questioned the need. "Come on, Commander!" he thought. "I mean, is all this truly necessary? Is this wave really that large? I mean, how big can it be?"

As a pilot with a vast amount of flying time under his belt, Dave Neel knew in his heart what the problem was: Watson just didn't want to alter the rhythm or break the spell he'd been so successful with, or leave Captain Singh and Aaron Bean exposed on deck a moment longer than absolutely necessary.

The H-60 has tons of power, and calling upon that awesome capability now, Neel and Watson began climbing fast, going straight up.

Perched in the aircraft's doorway, Brian Lickfield continued to winch up the seventh survivor. The sailor dangling in midair on the end of the hoist cable got quite a ride, too, as he went from the deck to a height of well over seventy feet in "just a couple of seconds."

"Man approaching cabin," Lickfield reported. "Basket's coming into the cabin. Man's in the cabin."

As the H-60 continued to rise, Dave Neel relinquished control of the aircraft back to Doug Watson.

"All right!" put in Watson. "I've got it! I've got it!"

The chopper was rising over the top of the giant cranes on deck, and the sodium lights mounted along the ends of the wheelhouse more than one hundred feet above the sea, when the H-60's "windshield went white" with foam. This was closely followed by a heavy, slapping sound.

Dave Neel's mind raced to identify something he'd never seen before from inside the cockpit of a helicopter. It was as if a semi-truck had just driven past and a wintery glomp of wet slush had blown off the top of its canopy, striking the windshield of his car.

"What is that?" he asked himself. "Is that snow?"

Doug Watson was still silently questioning both the wisdom and necessity of making such a radical climb, when the windshield in front of him went white with foam. He experienced a brief period of silence as he tried to absorb the sight. For a few seconds, he found himself lost in a kind of sound-warp. He would remember seeing things, but was not necessarily hearing them.

It was the breakthrough clamor of Brian Lickfield's voice that jolted him out of it.

"Holy shit!" yelled Lickfield. "We've got white water in the cabin, sir! Up! Up! Up!"

The gravity of the events now taking place, and the innate sense of responsibility Watson had toward each of the ten souls on board the helicopter—as well as the heartrending love he felt for his wife Colleen and two-month-old son Addison back in Kodiak—all weighed heavily on him now. A substantial intellect, coupled with extensive training and experience, made him instantaneously cognizant of the life-and-death nature of the struggle that had just begun.

Watson heard Dave Neel say something, then saw the windshield go white. It was like riding inside a vehicle passing through a car wash, when the soapy water slops over the window before you, and suddenly you can't see anymore. Watson heard a horn going off, and saw some flashing red lights inside the cockpit, warning that the rpms of their main rotor blades were getting perilously low. And then another red light lit up and another blaring horn announced that the aircraft's stabilator, a system that automatically maintains altitude, had failed.

The low-rotor rpm light caught Watson's attention, and he glanced at the power turbine and rotor tachometer gauges. They were all sitting in the lower red range. Initially, it didn't register with him that his engines were going off-line, and he began to decrease collective to try and recover some rpms.

Hoping that it had been only a little "splash encounter," Doug Watson pushed the cyclic forward, eased off on the collective arm, and "lowered the nose." He intended to fly out of it. And as he did so he could feel Dave Neel working the controls in the same, identical manner. But when the pilots tried to pull power, there was nothing left.

Watson could feel the aircraft start to shudder. It began to jerk back and forth then, and produced a kind of "jostling feeling, as if someone were kicking the bottom of a chair you're sitting on."

When Brian Lickfield's moment of truth arrived, he was still perched on one knee in the side door opening. He had just yanked the seventh crewman from India inside the cabin, and was tipping the basket on its side to help the survivor climb out, when he heard something odd. It was the hollow, echoing sound a blowhole makes when a wave strikes a rocky, pocketed seashore, and trapped air releases, and it just went "whomp!"

Incredibly, it seemed to Lickfield, in spite of the aircraft's substantial altitude a wall of seawater blasted up inside the helicopter, washed through and over her rotor blades, and engulfed the H-60 from top to bottom. The strength of the blast was astounding. It was as if someone had turned a firehose on him, and he felt "humbled" by the phenomenon.

Then the aircraft's alarms began sounding and, listening over his radio headset, Lickfield heard the quick exchanges between Neel and Watson grow garbled. Shortly, the number-one engine on the left side flamed out. As it spooled down, it made the sound an incoming artillery round might make. Then quit altogether.

"Damn!" thought Lickfield. "There goes number-one engine!"

A couple of seconds later, the number-two engine also began to shut down.

"Oh, hell, we're done for!" concluded Lickfield, as the shuddering aircraft stalled in midair. "We're going swimming."

Dave Neel turned and glanced back over his right

shoulder. White water was pouring into the cabin through the side door of the rear compartment.

"Water's in the cabin, sir!" Lickfield reinterated. "Up! Up! Up!"

Neel grabbed the controls and tried to steady the staggering aircraft. "We're going to fly out of this," he told himself determinedly. "We're going to fly away from this ship and climb above whatever just hit us, and go talk about it and decide what to do next. And then we'll come back and finish this. But for now we're going to get the hell out of here!"

Instead, Neel felt the aircraft yaw to the left, saw the master caution panel lights flashing, and heard Doug Watson call out, "N.R! N.R.!" [watch rotor speed].

Instinctively, Neel shot a glance at their EPI (Engine Performance Indicator), which monitors the engine oil temperature, pressure, and overall health of the transmission. Everything was going off-line, from yellow to red. Still trying to pull power, Neel again attempted to climb. But it was no use. He could feel the stalled copter begin to descend. Tipping as it went, it slid down and to the left.

As her engines flamed out, the thirty-foot-long tail of the aircraft pivoted around counterclockwise. Spinning at 1,890 rpms, the eleven-foot-wide swath of her tail rotor blades struck the side of the freighter and disintegrated upon impact. Countless pieces went flying. The explosive event also sheared off the entire, fifteen-foot-long canted tail section of the aircraft.

By putting all the effort they could into pulling power at the right time, however, Dave Neel and Doug Watson had jointly managed to work into the wind. And by tapping into that source of energy, and simultaneously bleeding off the last vestige of the chopper's engine power, they were able to slow their rate of descent long enough to slip out from over the top of the ship itself. In so doing, they cleverly managed to cushion their aircraft's fall, and to sidestep the cataclysmic collision of their sixteen-thousand-pound aircraft with the steel surface of the ship's formidable deck.

Falling from an altitude of more than one hundred feet, such a violent impact would have been catastrophic. The life-snuffing waters of the Bering Sea would soon have its say as to who would and would not survive. But by shifting the aircraft's point of impact, Neel and Watson managed to buy all ten men on board the 6020 at least a temporary stay of execution.

Most helicopter crashes are violent in the extreme, and often involve multiple deaths with a kind of crematory finale. This crash, mercifully, did not. And as the eight-ton aircraft and the ten men trapped inside it plunged into the sea, Dave Neel was quite certain that "every single person on the helicopter survived the crash sequence. No one died during the crash itself."

EIGHT

In the minutes before the crash, Aaron Bean had worked diligently to prepare each crewman for hoisting, and to calm and position those still anxiously awaiting their turn. Now and then he glanced up to try and catch a glimpse of the H-60 to mentally mark its position.

Ignoring the dangers, Bean grabbed the fourth survivor and shoved him into the basket. A moment later, both man and basket flew into the air. Bean felt pleased by the success. A fifth survivor rose toward the tireless machine riding the restless winds above. And then another. That made it six in a row.

The seventh survivor rose from the deck, leaving only the ship's captain and himself behind. The man was standing at the hand railing, holding on to it with a death grip, when Bean called out to him.

"Captain!" he yelled, motioning to him. "Come here!"

But Captain Singh froze. He looked at Aaron Bean, and then he glanced out to sea. And then Aaron, too, spotted it: a truly monstrous wave rolling straight for them.

Once again, Bean called to the captain. "Let's go! Let's go!" he urged.

But the man refused to move.

The wave plowed into the ship's port side, right beside them. "And then it did what all big waves do when they run into a wall," recalls Bean. "They explode! And this huge wall of green seawater just jetted straight up into the air right in front of us." Rising perhaps as high as 150 feet into the air, the watery eruption jetted out and away as it followed the curve of the bow. The wind carried the colossal rooster tail aft of them, just missing both parties.

Then, Aaron Bean heard the sickening sound of the H-60's number-one engine shutting down, as the suffocating wall of salt water washed over it. Spinning at a steady 20,900 rpms, and producing 3,000 horsepower to the main driveshaft, the gas turbine engine's power dropped to nothing. A moment later, number-two engine died, issuing the same ballistic report. Aaron Bean looked up in time to see the 16,000-pound aircraft falling out of the sky.

"Oh, shit!" he exclaimed.

With the fifty-four-foot swath of the aircraft's main rotor blades spinning almost directly overhead, there wasn't time to get safely out of the way. Certain her blades were going to lop off both of their heads, Bean yelled to the captain, "Duck!"

Unable to alter the course of the wildly dramatic moment, Bean dove to the deck, rolled up into a fetal position and turned his back to the free-falling chopper. He placed his hands behind his head, closed his eyes, and "tucked in tight as that huge thing came down."

Bean heard the metallic clack of the helicopter's rotor blades impacting the hand railing and deck beside him in rapid-fire sequence. Chunks of metal scattered like shrapnel. When he looked up again, Aaron Bean could see nickel-coated pieces of the rotor blades washing down the sloping deck. The titanium tip of one of the aircraft's rotor blades was lying on the deck directly in front of him. Aaron Bean had survived the crash without a scratch.

The energetic young rescue swimmer leapt to his feet and raced over to check on the captain. He, too, appeared to have survived unscathed. Speaking English heavily accented with the flavor of his homeland of India, he inquired about the men who'd been on board the chopper.

"Are they okay? Are they alive?" he asked.

"No," Bean replied, certain of their outcome. "They're dead. They're all dead."

Captain Singh began to yell and race around, then,

calling out, "So what are we going to do? What are we going to do?"

"Look!" Bean shouted, pulling the captain close. "I'm scared, too, so just calm down!"

Gradually, then, Bean began to piece together what was taking place around him. He accomplished this largely through the use of his hearing. Until then, the roar of the H-60 hovering so close overhead had drowned out all else, but the moment the aircraft plunged into the sea he became aware of the startling sound the alarms were making on board the *Selendang Ayu*.

"Sir, what do those alarms mean?" Bean asked Singh, altering the focus of their conversation.

"The compartments are flooding!" shot back the wide-eyed captain, referring to the ship's cargo holds.

As a certified EMT, the one thing Aaron Bean didn't want was to become trapped in a situation that was unsafe, with no way to make it safe. Stranded now, without his wet suit, hood, fins, goggles, or gear, Bean knew there was probably no way to survive in the water.

So what were the facts? Dry suit or none, in such icy seas human beings started to lose the dexterity in their hands in just four minutes. As for the seven passengers who were immersed in the ocean water without the protection of a survival suit, their bodies were at that moment losing heat at thirty times the rate they would in air of the same temperature. There was no way their bodies would be able to keep up.

Bean knew that ten men were inside the helicopter when it went down. All of them had gone into the water. Most of them would die.

H-65 pilots Tim Eason and Rob Kornexl had been hovering off, intently observing the successive hoists by the crew of chopper 6020, when the wave struck.

Standing forty- to forty-five-feet high, and moving at close to forty-miles per hour, the monster wave carried within it the power of a locomotive. Yet it was almost invisible against the backdrop of darkness. Hovering above and behind the H-60, now just completing its hoists, the crew of the H-65 had been watching the action from on high, and did not glimpse the wave until just before it hit.

"Oh, God!" said Eason, when he first glimpsed it. "That's going to be a bad one."

The rogue wave plowed into the bow of the grounded, stationary target and erupted skyward, producing a spectacular wall of ocean spray. The prevailing direction of the wind carried the curtainlike veil of leaden spray over the comparatively tiny, embattled figure of the H-60 rising before them, enveloping the sixty-five-foot-long helicopter, rotor blades, cockpit, rear cabin, tail section, tail rotor and all, essentially swallowing the aircraft whole.

The mammoth wave seemed to wrap itself around the freighter's bow. "It came up and back," says Eason. "And just exploded into this monstrous wall . . . that washed over the helicopter, completely obscuring it for several seconds from our vision."

"Holy shit!" exclaimed Eason.

Eason could see Dave Neel and Doug Watson trying to fly out of it. But as their engines flamed out from the massive intake of water, the helicopter seemed to falter in midair. Then it began its descent.

As the H-60 started down, her propellers impacted the crest of the wave and the side of the ship simultaneously, fracturing into countless pieces that went scattering in every direction. But here, providence dealt Tim Eason a lucky hand, for as he moved in closer to see if anyone had survived and to begin hoisting, if possible, a chunk of one of the 6020's main rotor blades, perhaps twenty feet of it, went cartwheeling past the front of the H-65's windshield, just missing them.

Barely clearing the deck, Neel and Watson crash-landed the H-60 on the crest of the monster wave, which luckily, was still lapping well up on the freighter's side.

Flight mech Greg Gibbons did not watch the H-60's end. Certain that the aircraft was going to crash, he grabbed the rescue basket and began preparing it for the work he knew was about to begin.

"Rob, push down all my pins," Eason told Kornexl, referring to shutting down the numerous radio channels they'd been monitoring. "All I want to hear is Greg, right now. I don't want to hear any other radios."

In spite of all the amazing action that had just taken place, a state of composure prevailed amongst the crew of the H-65. Tim Eason found the scene unfolding before him intensely poignant, for at that moment he knew that he'd just watched people die, though he had no idea exactly whom. Quite possibly, it was friends of his, people he'd known and worked with.

But for Eason and his crew, it always came back to the training. The initial, gut-wrenching sense of calamity was quickly replaced with a strong dose of professional detachment, one that said, "We'll worry about that later. For now, however, let's just do the job that's in front of us."

Seconds later, when the H-60 finally rolled over, Eason was flying the chopper, Kornexl was communicating on the radio, and Greg Gibbons was busily preparing the rescue basket for hoisting.

"Rescue checklist part two for basket recovery of the survivors," said Eason.

"Rescue check, part two is ready," said Gibbons.

Eason was impressed with his flight mechanic's performance, for it seemed that Gibbons had the rescue basket rigged and ready "almost instantly."

In the midst of a truckload of emotion, yet using one of the most level, matter-of-fact tones imaginable under such circumstances, Rob Kornexl radioed the news to the *Alex Haley*.

"Coast Guard cutter *Alex Haley*," he began, "this is Coast Guard rescue 6513. The H-60 has crashed into the water."

There was a pause most would attribute to disbelief.

"Er, what?" replied the radioman aboard the *Alex Haley*. "Say again? Would you please repeat that?"

"Roger. This is Coast Guard rescue 6513. Coast Guard helicopter 6020 has crashed into the water. We are moving in to pick up survivors. Request all possible assistance."

Inside the dark interior of the *Alex Haley*'s wheelhouse, the seconds clicked slowly past. The room was filled with the soft-red luminescent glow coming from numerous instrument panels. Ten servicemen stood by silently listening, completely attentive, acutely aware. One could hear the intermittent banter of the H-65's crew talking to one another, the muffled impact of waves crashing outside, and the moaning of the wind careening through the cable rigging overhead.

Flight deck crew boss Dale Estilette had spent a lot of time around Kornexl on that particular Bering Sea deployment. He'd come to know him as "a really cool, calm kind of guy. Prior Army. He'd done a lot in helicopters."

Estilette was standing inside the aviation shack with several members of his crew, when Kornexl first reported the crash. One of his men turned to another and said, "What did he just say?"

Kornexl repeated the grim news. Then all radio traffic between the cutter and the H-65 Dolphin ceased. For Estilette and those gathered there, the world stood still.

As the H-60 Jayhawk plunged into the sea, Lt. Dave Neel broke the safety seal on the inside of the left door, grabbed the handle, and shoved it forward. This released the metal teeth that gripped the outside edge of the window and held it in place. Then, using the palm of his right hand, he punched it out. With his side window jettisoned, a frigid river of ocean water began flooding the aircraft's cockpit.

Next, Neel reached down and released his seat belt harness mechanism. He was in a hurry. Everything he had been taught about the H-60 led him to believe that the moment the aircraft hit the water, it would immediately begin to sink. Then he felt the helicopter start to roll over. As it went, he told himself, "Your training, pal. Pause now. Give it a few seconds to determine which way your buoyancy is carrying you. Then push in that direction."

Finally able to orient himself, Neel reached up, grabbed the nearest edge of the recently vacated window opening, and pulled himself out. His worse fear—as he swam out of the dark waters of the overturned cockpit and stroked toward the surface—was of getting hung up on some part of the sinking aircraft and drowning.

Dave Neel broke through into the raw Alaskan night sputtering water. He was greeted by a mountainous arena of wind-raked sea. The ocean water was ice cold. As he treaded it, he took in the glare of the *Selendang Ayu*'s mastlights. Huge, irregular waves moving through lifted and tossed him, then exploded against the freighter's side. Neel couldn't see anyone else nearby.

Upwind of him, he noticed the fuselage of the overturned Jayhawk helicopter drifting his way. It was moving around like a rolling turtle. Fearing that he might be caught between the metal body of the aircraft and the bare steel wall of the freighter, Neel thought, "Hey, I gotta get away from this thing, or it's going to crush me, or snag me and pull me down into Davy Jones's Locker right along with it!" And with that in mind, he began backstroking away as fast as he could.

His aviator's suit provided a certain amount of buoyancy, but the water was impossibly cold. His hands were growing numb fast, and the water sloshing around inside his helmet stung his scalp. Then he detected a pinhole leak in the left leg of his dry suit. He could feel a trickle of the icy liquid leaking inside at about knee level. He remembered his life vest, and reached for the toggle. He made several attempts before finally locating it. He gave it a yank. It inflated.

Broad, hull-busting waves broke repeatedly against the side of the freighter. At one point, he found himself on the crest of a wave looking down on the H-60 floating upside down in the water. The aircraft's long tail section was jutting out of the ocean at a thirty-degree angle. The very end of it had been sheared off, but the rest of it appeared relatively intact.

For a few seconds, as the current carried him along toward the pounding surf in the darkness beyond, Neel floated on his back and tried to gather himself. Close by, and looking forty to fifty feet high, the long, pivoting, side of the *Selendang Ayu* stretched as far as he could see in both directions. He studied the wall for several seconds. There were no handholds or ladders built into her side. The ship was painted red below the flat waterline, and black above—colors that revealed themselves, to a greater or lesser degree, depending upon the leap and roll of the ship.

"There's no way that I can climb up on that damned thing," he finally concluded. "So what are my options?"

The ocean breakers now bashing into the side of the ship looked immense. Catching a ride on the backs of the groundswells, he saw the storm waves repeatedly stagger the huge, defenseless freighter, rocking her heavily.

"Well," he thought, "you can try to swim out of this. No, the seas are too big, and you are too cold." He paused to think it through. "So now what are you going to do?"

With no effective way to climb aboard the *Selendang Ayu*, or to slow the surprising speed with which the ocean current was carrying him into the surf zone, Neel felt doomed. Certain that he was a dead man, he decided to make his peace with God. He harbored some deep regrets. At home back in Kodiak, his wife Rose, daughters Diana and Madeline—ages ten and fourteen—were counting on his safe return, and his son Jack was just seven months old now. It was truly horrible to think that he'd never get to know the boy, or see him grow up.

Then he experienced something that he "never would have believed." He saw his life literally flash before his eyes. Yet he remained unafraid. He and Rose had developed a solid, spirit-filled connection to their Christian faith, and sincerely believed in the promise of the hereafter.

Although Dave Neel wasn't afraid to die, neither was he quite ready, just yet, to call in the hounds and give up the hunt. At one point as he drifted, he found himself on the upside of a swell, looking down on the white underside of his crashed helicopter as it floated along. He could see the letters USCG stenciled in black across her belly. Far more troubling was the fact that he hadn't seen anybody else swim out of the wreckage. His heart sank at the thought, and he asked himself, "Didn't anyone else make it out of that helicopter alive?"

"Okay," said Tim Eason, spotting the bobbing head of someone who'd managed to escape from the ruins of the downed helicopter. "There's our first survivor. Con me in."

Flying high over the bow of the *Selendang Ayu,* with her huge sodium mastlights "lighting up everything," Eason moved into position. Though surrounded by darkness, he would do his best to remain inside the pocket of light. Considering what they had just witnessed, Eason and Kornexl remained a little apprehensive about the whole thing and quickly agreed that it would be far safer to hoist from a significantly higher midair platform than had their predecessors.

While Tim Eason fought to levitate and hold station from a height of two hundred feet above the water—possibly the highest hoisting platform ever attempted by an H-65 pilot—Greg Gibbons began conning him in. With the basket soon trailing a good seventy feet behind the chopper, Gibbons began maneuvering the forty-five-pound stainless-steel cage down through the windswept skies. The trick was to get it as close as possible to the survivor in such desperate straits in the water below, without clubbing him with it.

The focus of his complete attention, at that moment, just happened to be Dave Neel.

NINE

Dave Neel was sliding steadily toward the surf into the "break zone." He knew he'd been pretty close to start with, but he could hear the seas breaking, now, right behind him. The sound intensified steadily as he drifted closer, and caused him a good deal of anxiety because he knew what that meant.

"Well, this is it," he thought.

Cut off from the world, trapped in such primitive circumstances, Neel had nearly given himself up for dead when he heard a faint but somehow familiar sound above the howl and crash of the wind and waves.

"What's that noise?" he puzzled.

He was drifting along parallel to the huge steel side of

the *Selendang Ayu* when he spotted the H-65 far overhead. The high pitch of the copter had gone unnoticed up until then, because the aircraft was hovering so high and the winds were so strong. He could see the ocean spray speeding through the brilliantly lit columns of her twin searchlights.

"Holy God!" he thought, his spirits soaring at the sudden revelation. "I completely forgot! The H-65 is still out here! Thank God! Oh, thank God!"

Neel waved his arms to indicate that he was alive and conscious. His elation was immediately tempered by the knowledge that, due to its much smaller size, the H-65 did not carry a rescue swimmer and could only hold a couple of survivors.

A full minute passed, and still the chopper made no apparent effort to approach him. Neel waved his arms back and forth again to draw their attention. Another minute passed, and as the roar of the breaking surf began to pound in his ears, he asked himself, "When in the hell are they going to start?"

"Hey, guys," he called out, "I'm still alive down here! Now come down and save me!"

When he glanced up again, he spotted a strange-looking, snakelike figure rising vertically into the sky. It hung there undulating, shimmering in the light as the heavy slants of blowing spray bled off of it. The line extended so far overhead that he had to ask himself, "What the hell are they doing? Are they sending me a trail line [a flimsy and quite useless 5/8-inch-thick length of rope]?"

Dave Neel reached out reflexively and it was "like right there," just an arm's length away. As his hand closed on it, he realized that it was the steel hoist cable. Glancing over his left shoulder then, Neel spotted the rescue basket bobbing in the water beside him. Working from a height of some two hundred feet overhead, Greg Gibbons had planted it, right on target.

"Damn right!" he yelled.

Neel spun around, grabbed the basket, and turned it on its side for easy entry, but somehow he slipped out. So he pushed the basket straight down into the water and climbed in. Then, for the first time in his life, flight commander David Neel gave the thumbs-up to those watching over him, and was immediately jolted from the water.

The wind shrieked over him, and the rescue basket pivoted slowly as it rose, giving Neel a full perspective of the chaotic scene. It was an amazing sight. He took in the monstrous size of the freighter, and the lights of the support vessels twinkling on the black horizon. And now and then, as he swung back and forth over the threatening seas, he caught a glimpse of the demolished hulk of his helicopter floating along just below the surface.

Neel felt almost overwhelmed with emotion at the sight. Waves of shame, embarrassment, and fear swept over him. The truth was that he'd been the acting commander of an

H-60 Jayhawk helicopter carrying a load of ten people, both crew and passengers—nine of whom, on this night, had looked to him for the answers. He sensed the tragic nature of the incident, because he knew that a number of people, including Doug Watson and Brian Lickfield, had probably been killed.

"Man, I gotta try and help all I can out here, now," Neel told himself.

The moment Greg Gibbons pulled him inside the helicopter, Neel rushed to extricate himself from the basket. To make room for the others, then, he scurried out of the way, cramming himself as far back into the far corner of the cabin as he could get.

Like the others who were on copter 6020 when it crashed, the ride inside the descending aircraft was a frightful one. For flight mechanic Brian Lickfield, the sound of the copter's engines flaming out and spooling down brought with it a gut-wrenching fear.

As the rotor blades impacted with the deck and side of the freighter, Lickfield felt the helicopter shudder. Riding it down was like getting trapped "on a badass roller-coaster ride," complete with fluttering stomach and overamping emotions. Then it began to roll over, tipping nose first, and as it went a kind of sickening feeling rushed over him. The notion struck him that the fourteen years of training he'd been through was somehow not enough to prepare him for what was currently happening. But with wife Rebecca and his four sons at home back in Kodiak, he had a lot to live for.

The gunner's belt Lickfield wore around his waist was a leather strap similar to a weight lifter's belt—thick, about five inches wide, and wrapped around his midsection. Another cord kept him toggled to the frame of the helicopter itself. There was no way he could fall out. But with the rescue basket partially blocking the cabin doorway, and seven terrified sailors behind him hoping to find their way out of the overturned aircraft and gain the surface, one could easily become entangled.

In an attempt to raise the oxygen level in his blood and give himself an edge, Lickfield started taking in deep lungfuls of air, his last for some time. Then the chopper hit the water, and the sea rushed in. Lickfield gasped as the icy surge flooded over him. He went under, rolled completely upside down, and hung there, waiting. The impact wasn't enough to throw him. It was not as violent as he had expected, but the cold, rushing water felt very real to Lickfield, and he knew instinctively that the next few moments were crucial to his survival.

Suppressing the growing panic, he waited and allowed the helicopter to stabilize for a few seconds. Submerged then, he looked around but saw no one. Suspended in the suffocating darkness, Lickfield decided to begin by concentrating on what he absolutely had to do next.

First off, Brian Lickfield adamantly refused to leave his post. He remained there, steadfast, clutching the handle built into the main body of the chopper at shoulder level in the dark, inverted space. In spite of everything that was happening around him, he would remain at his post, exactly as trained, precisely where he was supposed to be.

Then, submerged in the murky, disorienting space, he saw the egress lights come on. The brilliant row of LED lights went all the way around the perimeter of the side door, completely encircling him. The gleaming little lights traced the rectangular-shaped exit with perfect clarity.

Lickfield held a joker card, an edge against the hazards of just such a predicament, one that he would call upon now. Throughout his lengthy career as a flight mech, he had always made it a point to put his harness belt on in exactly the same way. During the long years of training, and more training, and still more, and all the missions in between, whenever he'd dress down he'd take care to discipline himself, as part of his own extended code of safety, to always wear his gunner's belt around his waist in exactly the same way, with the quick-release mechanism on the right side of his abdomen.

In fact, during his extensive training, whenever he had

discovered that he'd donned it with the release on his left side, something that is perfectly acceptable even under the Coast Guard's own rules, he would always take it off and place it back on the right side. Just in case. Calling, now, upon this vow of consistency, Lickfield reached confidently down and hit the release on the right side of his gunner's belt, and he was free.

Seconds later, his head broke through the ocean surface. At that moment, Lickfield felt a brief exultation of spirit and screamed aloud, "YEH!" Then he looked up and took in the massive, pivoting face of the port side of the *Selendang Ayu*. The rocking, fifty-foot-high wall of steel seemed to stretch forever across the water, and extended out of sight. He was sliding past it now at an astonishingly fast clip, and was already some distance from the overturned shell of the copter. Barely afloat, and drifting along with its nose down at a much slower rate as it slid along the hull of the freighter, the 6020 would disappear now and then beneath the long, sweeping ground-swells and free-falling breakers.

His heart went out to anyone still trapped inside the helicopter. But without a wet suit, mask, snorkle, flippers, and scuba tank—accessories he didn't even own—there was no way Lickfield could swim back to the chopper, dive down, locate the side-door entrance several fathoms below, and remain there long enough to somehow guide them out. It was all he could do, now, just to stay afloat. Besides, as fast as his face, feet, and hands were going numb, he, too, would be lucky to survive. It was an impossible dilemma. And a gut-wrenching one, as well.

Upon impact with the water, some in back may have become paralyzed with fear. Others, encountering the breath-robbing shock of the icy sea, had no doubt panicked and, gagging on the cold rush of acrid ocean were, at that moment, struggling blindly in the suffocating darkness to somehow disentangle themselves from one another, locate the exit, and live.

But inverted as they were, the floor had now become their ceiling, and the ceiling their floor, and the cabin door opening they all hoped to gain now stood on the opposite wall of the darkened cabin. And with the 6020 floating with her nose pointed down into the depths as she was, the buoyancy of the cumbersome block life preservers the seven sailors wore had likely carried them back into the far reaches of the cabin and pinned them there. It was a place from which they stood almost no chance of escaping.

Additionally, the hard truth was that all through his rescue training Brian Lickfield had been taught that if he were so unbelievably lucky enough to survive a helicopter crash, he was to "get out and not to go back. To *never* go back. Because that's when people die!" Regrettably, for now, it was every man for himself.

Lickfield scanned the face of a passing wave for other

survivors, but "the seas were huge" and crested repeatedly over him, and he found himself forced to swim for his life.

Nor would he survive for long in the frigid waters of the far north without the kind of thermal protection a survival suit provides. He wouldn't have to worry about dying from hypothermia, though, because there wasn't time. The waves and currents forcing him so briskly along would soon carry him into a surf that lay completely hidden, though not at all silent, in the darkness beyond the stern, and that would be that. There was no way one could swim against it.

"I'm not out of this yet," Lickfield observed, serving upon himself the brutal reminder. Again it struck him that he'd be very lucky to survive his present predicament at all. "I could still die out here," he thought. "I'm in the goddamned Bering Sea now in thirty-five-foot seas!"

With the sickening odor of the JP-5 fuel now filling his nostrils, Lickfield began swimming against the current anyway. He was sidestroking along, and tiring quickly in his cold, unprotected state, when he caught sight of Dave Neel out of the corner of his eye. Neel was about thirty feet away. It was only a brief sighting. The two men did not wave, speak, or make physical contact. In fact, Neel never saw him.

Lickfield was relieved to know that his commander was still alive, though he could clearly see that it was

already a struggle for him just to swim. Then a wave rico-
cheted off the hull, and a jetting ridge of spin-off sea carried
Dave Neel away.

Brian Lickfield was determined to see his lovely wife
Becky and their four boys again. There was Daniel, two;
Joe, eight; Alex, eleven; and Robert, thirteen. He needed
to keep his head above water and try, somehow, to slow
his rate of drift as he waited for help to arrive. But then he
began gagging reflexively on the JP-5 fuel leaking from
the wreckage of the helicopter. The buoyant, oil-based fuel
was being blown across the top of the water, and was
repeatedly coating his body. The smell of it was almost
suffocating.

He was choking on it, and trying to swim, when a big
storm wave ran him over. The free-falling tonnage of the
sneaker wave slammed him hard. It drove him under and
seemed quite determined to drown him there on the spot.
Fighting his way to the surface, he struggled to catch his
breath and remain afloat.

Now and then, as Tim Eason guided the H-65 ahead into
the oncoming winds, Rob Kornexl would call out their
altitude. Equally important to keep in mind, Eason knew,
was that the *Selendang Ayu* had run aground only about
a thousand feet from the cliff-lined shores of Unalaska
Island. The seas below them were drafting the bobbing

survivors along at a surprisingly fast clip, sucking them toward a kill zone of white water and growling surf.

As a consequence, Tim Eason was repeatedly forced to slide back on the wind in an effort to remain abreast of them. Eventually, he found himself flying around the vessel's tall, white wheelhouse.

With the darkness now hiding the rugged coastline behind him, and the roar of their chopper muting the sounds of the storm waves thundering ashore, Eason turned to his co-pilot.

"Hey, Rob, where are those cliffs?"

"I got it," Rob Kornexl assured him. "Don't worry. I've got it."

"All right. But it still worries me a little."

With Dave Neel now safely aboard, Greg Gibbons sent the basket back out the door.

Flight mechanic Brian Lickfield soon realized that he was working much harder to remain afloat than he should have. "At this rate," he thought, "I won't last for long." Then it struck him. He reached down and pulled the toggle cord on his life vest. He was pleased to hear the sound of his CO_2 cartridge discharge, and relieved to feel its buoyancy lifting him.

Intermittently blindsided by sneaker waves, and gagging on jet fuel, Lickfield's experience, as he drifted along, was wretched. As the minutes passed, he could feel the insidious chill of the water pressing in on him. He was growing tired, a symptom of hypothermia. Futile as it seemed, he kept swimming doggedly along to slow his rate of drift—vitally important if he hoped to be seen in the growing darkness.

He'd about given himself up for dead when "out of nowhere" the rescue basket plopped down in the water close by. Hoisting from that exceptional height, flight mech Greg Gibbons had, once again, hit his mark.

In his confused state, Lickfield thought he might have actually been holding his own against the prevailing currents, though in such mountainous seas it was difficult to tell, precisely. In truth, however, by the time Gibbons had completed the almost surgical delivery of the H-65's rescue basket, Lickfield had drifted nearly the full length of the freighter.

The helicopter was up there somewhere, but Lickfield found that with the JP-5 jet fuel blurring his vision he couldn't focus on it at all. Rimmed with bright red foam collars on either end, the rescue basket was floating upright in the water. For Lickfield, it was an amazing moment. He grabbed the basket with both hands in a death grip, and thanking God that he was still alive, rolled inside it butt-first. Then, squinting into the light far overhead, he gave the thumbs-up sign, and yelled, "Let's go!"

Both man and basket had just begun to drift down into the yawning canyon of another deep wave trough when Gibbons lifted him clear of the water and began reeling him in. Lickfield felt an immediate sense of relief, and thrilling to the moment, he thought, "YES! I'm going to LIVE!"

The basket carrying him pivoted slowly in the force-9 winds, and as he rose he caught a glimpse of the ruins of the H-60 out of which he'd just swum. "It was just starting to sink, which is crazy," he would later recall, "because the 60 is made of steel and aluminum. It's a very fast-sinking helicopter. You can expect it to sink at a rate of six or seven feet per second. But that 6020 floated for damned near fifteen minutes!"

Greg Gibbons pulled the rescue basket in through the side door and dumped Brian Lickfield out on the floor. With years of crewing on an H-65 under his belt, Lickfield knew exactly where to find the ICS (Inter-Com System) cord. He grabbed it and plugged it into his helmet so he could listen to the pilots converse. They were talking about Aaron Bean, the rescue swimmer. They had assumed he was on the 6020 when it crashed and had since gone missing. They were desperately trying to locate him, and the others as well.

Lickfield tried to tell them that Bean was hanging tough and still looking after the last remaining survivor, the ship's captain, on the bow of the freighter. But there was water in his mic and they were unable to understand anything he was saying. So he leaned forward, grabbed Greg Gibbons by the shoulder, and yelled into his ear.

"Aaron and the captain are still on the boat!" he said, news which Gibbons quickly passed on to the pilots up front.

Far below them now, Lickfield could see the helicopter drifting along just under the surface, with debris floating past. He also sighted another survivor in the water, someone still caught up in the struggle. Somehow, he'd managed to escape the H-60 and endure the heart-stopping cold.

That person just happened to be Doug Watson.

TEN

When his helicopter plummeted into the sea Watson did not feel any kind of significant impact. The experience was very similar to that of riding the simulator back at the base in Mobile, Alabama. It took about a second for the torrent of ocean water rushing in through the cabin door to fill his cockpit. The flood of salt water brought with it the immediate cessation of all electronic communications.

Like the rest of his crew he wore a thin Coast Guard dry suit, one lined with a heat-retaining layer of fleece. With flight boots covering his feet and watertight seals built into the ankles, wrists, and neck, only his face and hands came in direct contact with the heat-robbing cold of the Bering Sea.

Doug Watson tried to prepare himself for the frozen blast. With his heart pounding in his chest, he took a deep breath and held it. He was so psyched up in anticipation of the shock that when the moment of truth actually arrived, he was somewhat surprised, because he thought that, initially, the water would actually feel colder than it did.

Hanging upside down, however, still strapped in his seat, Watson was unable to assist the others. The seven sailors whom he and his crew had just hoisted aboard, were no doubt fighting to locate the exit in the rear cabin at that very moment. Like he and crewmates Dave Neel and Brian Lickfield, each of them would have to find his own way out.

Watson could make out the blurry red instrument lights pulsing on the dashboard before him. But inverted as he was in the murky space, he couldn't really discern which lights they were.

Like all pilots, every year Doug Watson had to pass an emergency egress procedure. This training is carried out in the controlled environment of a swimming pool. Strapped into the chair inside a simulated cockpit, each pilot is turned upside down so that, completely submerged, they can experience a similar crisis and practice their escapes.

Watson's training dictated a set number of specific steps for a pilot to follow to exit his or her downed helicopter. He knew them well. They came to him in order now, automatically, like a reflex. He started with Step #1, which is "Wait for all motion to stop."

Pausing, then, he felt the aircraft roll the rest of the way over. Then his ears started popping. Which made sense, because he'd been taught that if a pilot were forced to ditch an H-60 in water, it would immediately begin sinking at a rate of "something like seven feet per second into Davy Jones's Locker." In fact, he was quite certain that he and anyone else still trapped inside the H-60 were, at that moment, sinking like a stone toward the bottom.

Understandably, he was in a bit of a rush to get out. Yet in spite of this, he forced himself to sit tight for several seconds. Step #2 dictated that he "Find a reference point." Locating the handle used to open the cockpit door beside him was essential. Under normal conditions, he could have easily located it by reaching down alongside his right ankle, just below the knee. Now, however, he knew it would be positioned in that airless, inverted space directly overhead.

Watson was also aware that the last thing a pilot wanted to do at such a time, was to release his seat belt and shoulder harness before he had located the door handle. He knew if he did, he'd start free-floating and swimming around inside the cockpit. Disoriented, unable to find his way out, he'd be lost.

He was completing Step #3—undoing the cords from

his helmet and intercom system—when it struck him that he was running out of oxygen. It was time to access the miniature oxygen tank that was attached to his life vest.

"Slow your mind down," Watson told himself, remaining steadfast against the panicky, fight-or-flight mentality. "Stand your ground and concentrate on what you need to do next to get out of here." Once he had diverted the panic, Watson felt an immediate sense of relief.

In truth, however, he was running out of oxygen. Yet he couldn't remember which step in the checklist called for him to secure his oxygen bottle. (There is no specific emergency training step for this.)

So, Watson reached for his HEED (Helicopter Emergency Egress Device) bottle. This "little scuba tank" was about the size of a twenty-ounce bottle of water and had approximately three minutes of breathable air inside it. A lanyard connects the cap of the tiny air tank to the pilot's vest. Gripping the bottle with his right hand, Watson extended it out to arm's length in the dark water in front of him. He did this several times to make sure the cap was off. But when he attempted to slip the mouthpiece between his lips something kept blocking the way, and he was eventually forced to concede a temporary defeat.

Unable to access his supply of oxygen, he dropped the HEED bottle and again began feeling around for the door handle. But once more he was unable to locate it. "Okay," he told himself, as his need for air became more acute, "I'm going to need some of that oxygen, now." Abandoning the search for the door handle, he quickly relocated his bottle and tried yet again, to fit its breathing nozzle into his mouth. But he still "couldn't for some reason."

With the need to breathe increasing by the second, Watson felt a growing sense of urgency to either find a way to access the air inside his oxygen bottle, or locate the door handle and make his escape.

"Okay," Watson figured, "I need to go back and refocus on the door handle again." Dropping the air bottle, he began searching the darkness, feeling his way along. He became aware, as his need escalated, that he was not really concentrating. He was certain that he'd "already touched the door handle without actually feeling it."

"Screw it!" thought Watson, finally. "I need that air bottle!"

He quickly relocated the HEED bottle, carefully felt the mouthpiece with his forefinger to make sure the cap was off, and then began mashing the mouthpiece against his lips. The visor on his helmet, he finally realized, had been blocking his attempts all along. This time he was able to slip the regulator past it and into his mouth. Using the last of the air in his lungs, he blew out a little bit to purge and prime the mouthpiece. Then he took a small,

cautious breath to make sure all the seawater had been
flushed out of it. Finally free to breath, Doug Watson in-
haled the precious oxygen ravenously.

Shortly thereafter, Watson's right hand chanced upon
the door handle above him. Then, mentally, he proceeded
with the steps to egress the aircraft.

"Open the door," he thought. "Disconnect the intercom cord attached to your helmet. Undo your seat belt
and shoulder harness. Then walk yourself hand over
hand to the exit and pull yourself through."

Watson could feel the surging force of the sea rocking
the helicopter. He pulled down on the handle and shoved
out on it. The door had opened only about a foot when he
slipped through the gap and struck out for the surface.
He was surprised to discover how close it was. Gulping
air, he came up alongside the drifting hulk of the H-60.
Like fellow crew members Dave Neel and Brian Lickfield
before him, he took in the long metal stub of her tail section protruding from the sea, and the enormous wall of
the freighter stretching toward the stern.

Drafted along by the tidal currents, Watson could also
hear the mounting roar of the nearby surf. As he drifted
ever closer, he got caught short by a couple of breaking
waves, thirty-footers or better that barreled right over
him. They tossed him about like so much flotsam.

Another comber roared down upon him, flipping him
through the depths. But his jumpsuit proved buoyant

enough, and when he surfaced again he drew in deep lungfuls of the damp night air. He was trying to gather himself
when the crown of yet another storm wave crashed down
upon him. He took a deep breath and held it. The wave
sent him tumbling. The cold currents stung his face.

Doug Watson regained the surface, thankful that he
had not been drowned on the spot. Through it all, as he
drifted down into the deep, valleylike wave troughs and
up over their tall, unpredictable crests, he looked intently
for other survivors, but never glimpsed a soul.

Several minutes passed before he remembered that he
wore an inflatable life vest. Pulling on the cord attached
to it, he popped the CO_2 cartridge. His vest filled almost
instantly.

Now Watson performed a quick self-assessment. He
knew he wasn't seriously injured, but he was also aware
that he was getting progressively colder, and that he could
do almost nothing about it. How long could a man last in
such cold water? Five minutes? Ten? Twenty? There was
no way to know for sure. But all that really didn't matter,
now, because at the pace the currents were sweeping
him along, they would soon deliver him into that fearsome
no-man's-land of cruel surf lying dead ahead.

Then he heard the noise of a helicopter working the
skies above. Watson couldn't actually see the aircraft itself—
like Lickfield before him, his vision had become blurred by
all the JP-5 fuel washing over him—but he felt it was almost

certainly Tim Eason's H-65. If so, with ten people in the water, the smaller copter wouldn't be able to take them all. They'd have to make several trips.

Doug Watson was also quite certain that if the crew of the H-65 overhead did not get him soon, he'd no longer be there when they got back. The stern of the ship seemed to grow progressively larger now. Drafted along by the swift tidal currents, he hung on.

Like the others, Watson could hear with increasing clarity the thundering reverberations of the fearsome surf. He knew the blackest darkness awaited anyone venturing there. Driven by waves packing hundreds of tons of bone-crushing power, he'd be mashed like a bug against the rock cliffs awaiting him, or be disemboweled when the ocean breakers flung him against barnacle-covered surf rocks, some the size of dump trucks. Either way, he was quite certain that he stood no chance of surviving such a meat grinder.

Then, as he was being drafted up the face of another large groundswell, Watson spotted a strobe light blinking off to his right. But he couldn't make out whether the light was attached to one of his own crewmen, or one of the sailors off the *Selendang Ayu.*

At about that same time, Doug Watson spotted another strobe light nearby. How many people were in the water? Were any of the others still alive? He'd only seen the two for certain, when the all-consuming gleam of the

H-65's twin searchlights found him. By the time Tim Eason flew into position at altitude, and Greg Gibbons once again applied his deft touch to the hoisting, Watson had drifted nearly to the stern.

He was reaching for the rescue basket floating nearby when he spotted one of the crewmen of the *Selendang Ayu* across the way. The man had somehow managed to swim out of the wreckage of their overturned chopper wearing one of the freighter's old cork-block life preservers. Instead of climbing inside, Watson grabbed the rescue basket in one hand, and immediately began dragging it along behind him, sidestroking through the water and over the mountainous seas toward the floating form of the lone survivor.

Several times as he swam along, Watson could feel the basket practically getting jerked out of his hands. He was certain, as he rode over the soaring peaks and down into the broad, sweeping wave troughs between breakers, that Greg Gibbons was having to work diligently to keep it near him. As he struggled along, he noticed that his hands were growing numb and unresponsive far more quickly than he'd anticipated. The sailor wearing the impossibly cumbersome and outdated life preserver was facing away from Watson when he swam up. As he drew close to the man, he began splashing water and calling out to him, trying to get his attention.

"Hey, pal, it's time to go!" Watson yelled.

He could not see the sailor's face, and the sounds of the wind and surf combined with the noise of the helicopter hovering overhead were so loud that his words were quickly drowned out. Then, tossed by a passing whitecap, the crewman in the life preserver rolled toward him. Watson could see that he was completely unresponsive. His eyes were open and fixed, frozen in a vacant deathstare.

The movement of the water and the motion of the helicopter made the basket jerk, once again, in Watson's hand. He remained keenly aware then that "those guys were up there working their butts off for me, and were probably having a real hard time of it." He needed to expedite his part of the rescue effort.

In the cockpit of the H-65 battling to hold station overhead, Tim Eason picked up on his headset the voice of Greg Gibbons talking to himself under his breath in the rear cabin. The ballsy flight mech seemed to be trying, by sheer willpower, to coax Doug Watson into the basket several hundred feet below.

"Just get into the basket, Doug," he said quietly. "Just get into the goddamned basket!"

It was then that Tim Eason witnessed the white underbelly of the overturned helicopter finally sink. As it disappeared into the depths, the hydraulics bay shield, the big

C-shaped cover mounted in front of the rotor head, came floating to the surface. Illuminated as it was in the center of Eason's personally controlled searchlight, the vision proved to be a "surreal moment" for him.

Exhausted from the effort, Doug Watson knew intuitively that he couldn't delay his own rescue much longer. He spotted yet another sailor from the freighter drifting off to his right, thirty or forty feet away, but knew he wouldn't be able to make it to him. Stiff from the cold, Watson pulled the rescue basket close and crawled clumsily inside it. A microsecond later, Greg Gibbons yanked him clear of the sea.

When Watson arrived inside the chopper, the first thing he noticed was that David Neel and Brian Lickfield were both present and alive. He was gladdened by the sight, but at the same time he kept thinking that Aaron Bean was still in the water. He'd completely forgotten that they had lowered him onto the bow of the foundering freighter shortly before they crashed. No one thought to remind him. So he continued to believe that he had, quite tragically, lost Aaron.

ELEVEN

Aaron Bean was standing on the foredeck of the *Selendang Ayu* with his feet widespread, braced against the waist-deep rivers of cascading seawater that often came rushing around the eight-foot-high, fifty-foot-square islands of the cargo holds, and raced down the otherwise unobstructed portions of the deck. Yet he never let the ship's captain out of his sight. Imperfect as it was, Bean had found a bit of protection from the storm for the two of them in the lee of the fo'c'sle wall, under a steel lip that extended out horizontally for several feet from the bow deck just overhead.

The foredeck stood nine or so feet above the main deck. The space between those two decks is known as

the fo'c'sle. Depending upon the type of ship, inside it
are separate compartments or holding areas where the
Herculean-sized anchor chains are stored whenever the
ship is under way. On the many king crab boats that still
ply those same waters around Unalaska Island, towlines,
canned food stuffs, tools, or shots of crab-pot line are
stored there. But should the vessel capsize, anyone caught
inside such a dank, rusty, airless space would be trapped.
In short, inside the bow compartment of the fo'c'sle on a
foundering vessel was definitely not the place to be.

Now, with Captain Singh's safety momentarily assured,
Aaron Bean turned on his emergency strobe light and attached it to a strip of Velcro on his helmet. The light, which
was set to flash every ten seconds or so, was the signal for
"In trouble! Need assistance!" Though hardly news to anybody, by displaying it prominently the blinking strobe light
would prove useful to those hovering aloft trying to keep
track of him and the captain.

In his mind, now, Aaron Bean worked to compartmentalize the problems he faced. His crewmates who had gone
into the drink were, at the very least, injured or presently
struggling to survive. He had to concede that the crash
had probably killed them. But he also knew that there was
absolutely nothing that he could do to assist them. They
were highly trained military men. None of them would go
down without a fight. The H-65 did not carry a rescue

swimmer, but he knew that Eason and the boys would do everything possible to recover any survivors.

Bean was also aware that he, too, was in grave danger. His survival gear was on the H-60 when it augered in, and had gone into the drink right along with his crewmates. Also, as the *Selendang Ayu* rolled to and fro in such extremes it sometimes appeared to be a hundred-foot drop from the upper railing to the ocean's surface. There was no way to make such a colossal leap unscathed. Jump overboard at the lower end of the hull's heaving cycle, and in the next round of heave-ho, she would likely roll back and crush him.

And even if he and the captain somehow managed to safely enter the water, where would they go? Should the ship roll over, dumping them into the sea, he'd be unable to effect a swimmer's rescue for long. In spite of his training and exceptional physical condition, Aaron Bean would be positively unable to withstand the steady and insidious encroachment of hypothermia for any significant length of time without his reserve swimmer's dry suit and hood, mask, snorkle, and fins.

The tides in that area fluctuate as much as twenty-five feet, and the currents are powerful enough to carry away even the world's fastest swimmer. Once, several decades before, a young Coastie named Jon Norgaard, a Quarter-Master Petty Officer 3rd Class, was piloting the 255-foot

World War II steam-electric weather ship *Wauchusett* through nearby Akutan Pass. Running with the tide, the ship, traveling at seventeen and half knots, caught a ride on a seventeen-knot tidal current and reached a top speed of thirty-four and a half knots (approximately forty mph) during the crossing that day.

Momentarily leaving the fo'c'sle area, and the discipline of his self-imposed tasking, Bean allowed himself to peer over the side, and scanned the scene of the crash. He caught sight of the white underside of his H-60 being carried away on the currents. Dwarfed by the dimensions of the waves crashing over the top of it, the orange-striped aircraft rode along with its round, black "bumblebee nose" pointing down into the depths.

Designed to deploy automatically in such calamities, the aircraft's landing gear was fully extended now, standing bolt upright, tires at the ready, dangling in midair. One moment the tires would disappear beneath the surge of a passing wave, then they would emerge for a time as the peak of the swell moved on.

Hurrying back to his duties, Bean plied Captain Singh with a number of quick-fire questions. He wanted to know why all the alarms were going off, and why no one on board had been wearing a survival suit.

"Do you have a radio?" Bean asked.

"Yes," replied the captain. He pulled it from his pocket and started yelling over the radio.

"Selendang Ayu! Selendang Ayu!"

Someone aboard the Coast Guard cutter *Alex Haley* cut in matter-of-factly. "Sir, you're going to have to calm down."

"Give me the radio," ordered Bean. Singh complied. "Coast Guard cutter *Alex Haley*! Coast Guard cutter *Alex Haley*!" Bean began. "The helicopter 6020 is in the water. The rescue swimmer and the ship's captain are still on board the *Selendang Ayu*. Over."

"Roger," came the reply. "Good copy. Understand."

Bean hiked back over to the hand railing to take another look. Squinting against the salty spray and cold, eye-watering force of the wind, he spotted two Coast Guardsmen floating over the brutish waves. Their CO_2 vests were inflated. He could make out the shape of their helmets, and the bright orange of their survival suits, with several brilliant bars of retro tape reflecting back at him.

Then a third Coastie surfaced on the opposite side of the overturned chopper. All three were swimming on separate paths away from it. Seeing no sign of any of the seven crewmen from India who'd been riding inside the chopper when it crashed, Bean rushed back to Captain Singh. He was still standing, dripping wet and shaking, where Bean had left him, beside the wall of the fo'c'sle compartment.

Relatively new to Kodiak, this was Aaron Bean's first rescue mission on the high seas. Aside from notions of fear that occasionally fluttered in his belly, he was feeling pretty juiced up. His senses were heightened. His body was tight; his thoughts, very sharp. He made the conscious decision to stay in the present moment and not go off on some emotional jag over things he could not control. He'd focus on those things he knew he was absolutely obliged to do. He'd look after the ship's captain. Period. That, he reminded himself, was his calling.

He checked to see if his strobe light was functioning properly. Then he decided to try to locate a safer place for both of them to ride out the storm. The two men began to move toward the wheelhouse. Perhaps it would be better to make a stand there. Certainly the ride would be smoother, and the shelter inside it far superior. But they'd hardly begun when Bean noticed how the rampaging storm waves were breaking over the deck, cargo holds and all. Foaming rivers of white water were jetting out from between these holds, racing from port to starboard, all along the yawning expanse of the deck stretching before them.

The amount of water crashing aboard usually depended upon the chance timing between the tilt of the freighter's deck, and the arrival of the next incoming wave. Sometimes wave water as much as twelve feet deep would come rolling aboard and go tearing down the steep, thirty-five-degree slope of the teetering deck. Dashing up against the hatch covers, the unstoppable tonnage of the rampaging flood would create geysers of erupting sea, before shooting out through starboard hand railings, over the side, and out into space.

The sight forced Bean to reexamine the extreme nature of the dangers that he and the captain were facing, and the odds of surviving such an odyssey. The hike involved traversing a deck that was nearly six hundred feet long. Bean knew that should one of the sneaker waves barreling aboard catch them out in the open, they probably wouldn't survive it. They'd taken only a few steps when he concluded that such a transit was most definitely not in their best interest.

"No-no-no!" Bean cautioned, as he escorted Singh back to their original hideout. "No way! We're staying here, sir! No way!"

Clad in nothing more than everyday street shoes and office-worker clothing, Captain Kailash Singh stood only five feet nine, weighed about 145 pounds, and spoke with a heavy Indian accent. Although it was difficult to follow his broken English, Bean could usually decipher what the man was trying to say.

As the storm intensified, so much wave water began to find its way up on deck that even in the fo'c'sle area waist-deep deluges of storm-driven sea came flooding in. To Aaron Bean, the runoff sprinting down the open deck between the fo'c'sle wall and the nearest cargo hold looked like it had been shot from a fire hydrant. Even the rapids of the mighty Colorado River did not run that fast. And each time one of these freshets of sea came rushing their way, Singh would literally climb the pipes on the side of the bulkhead to try to keep his feet and legs from being further numbed by the rushing waters.

"I cannot swim! I cannot swim!" he announced.

Bean did his best to reassure him.

"Look, sir, I am a rescue swimmer," he said. "And if we have to go into the water, I won't let go of you. I'll hold on to you."

The hard truth, as Aaron Bean saw it, was that even with all the aid he could personally muster, if they were forced into the water the captain wouldn't last for long. But regardless, Bean's innate sense of duty would still not allow him to leave the man and swim off. He would never abandon the captain. He'd place him in a controlled, cross-chest carry and remain with him and try to keep him afloat until they were rescued, or until he himself died. Secretly, the young rescue swimmer gave the captain from India about ten minutes. Himself, slightly longer.

Standing with knees bent, and feet shoulder-width apart, Bean faced each new burst of deck surf with one hand on the pipe and the other on the bulkhead, all the while keeping a sharp eye peeled for those huge, punishing waves that, again and again, drove so forcefully into the side of the freighter, and broke over the handrails, several stories above.

Grounded on the runway back in Cold Bay, Pat Bacher and Doug Cameron were busily checking out their H-60 Jayhawk, when fellow pilot Guy "Yogi" Pierce came running up holding the Cold Bay Lodge's telephone in his hand.

"We need to launch right now!" he began. "Because we just heard the 6020 has crashed into the sea!"

"Sorry, Yogi," replied Doug Cameron, hardly able to believe the rotten luck. "This plane is broken hard. There is no way we can launch with it tonight."

Like everyone on the ground there in Cold Bay, Cameron felt just horrible about the situation. He knew the wives and kids of each of the men on board the downed aircraft quite well. But there was nothing to be done. Having just left the rescue site, Cameron knew firsthand how huge the waves were, how cold the water was, and had seen the man-eating surf that awaited them, and he was quite certain, now, that everyone who'd been riding the 6020 at the time of the crash was dead.

Eventually, observing the standard radio guard protocol, Rob Kornexl contacted the *Alex Haley* and gave a brief ops and position report.

"Our flight operations are normal," he said. He followed this with a quick rundown of the basic facts, including sea conditions. He reported that there was bunker oil leaking into the water. They had recovered three survivors, and were searching for more.

The second that Greg Gibbons finished hoisting Doug Watson aboard, Tim Eason nosed the H-65 Dolphin back into the action. Remaining totally focused on the moment, he applied a learned hand to the controls in an attempt to maintain something akin to a stationary hover, in order to avoid being swept into the pivoting path of one of the sixty-foot-high deck crane towers, or get Sunday-punched by an unexpected blast from a williwaw accelerating down the slopes of nearby Makushin Volcano.

With Neel, Watson, and Lickfield safely aboard, Gibbons remained ready at a moment's notice to apply his considerable savvy to the challenges at hand. His fourth hoist, however, would prove to be a bit more complicated.

It involved a gentleman named Rajiv Dias, a crewman from India and a cadet on the *Selendang Ayu*. Having spied the man drifting near the stern of the freighter, Gibbons began conning Tim Eason into position. After several efforts amid all the intense winds, he somehow managed to land the basket quite close to the sailor. Without the protection of a survival suit, however, Dias had become nearly catatonic from the cold. As Gibbons watched, he made one clumsy attempt to climb inside the basket, then fell backward into the sea, apparently unconscious. If the man was still alive, little time remained. Floating in such a nonresponsive state, he was being swept quickly along into the kill zone.

With no rescue swimmer on board the H-65, and no other options left to him, Greg Gibbons devised a plan. He would go fishing with the rescue basket. His plan was to try to use the basket as a kind of makeshift ladle. The audacious winch man would attempt to literally scoop up the dying man, plucking him out of the sea.

Tim Eason brought the aircraft down into a tenuous hover about 150 feet above the unconscious crewman. The H-65 was getting "kicked around pretty good, too," he recalls, as Gibbons conned him "first left, and then right, and back and then forward." And as he did, turbulent fifty- and sixty-knot winds whiplashed them. Yet, somehow in the midst of the elemental chaos, Gibbons once again managed to bring the basket down and drop it in the water right beside Dias.

"Sir," Gibbons eventually reported to Tim Eason, "he won't get in. And I can't shake him off." Dias, it seemed, had somehow become entangled with the hoist cable on the outside of the basket itself.

"Well, I'll tell you what, Greg," said Tim Eason. "We've got to have that basket back. Aaron Bean and the captain are both still on board the ship there. The captain's stable. But we're going to have to get them both soon." He paused. "So I'll come down to one hundred feet, and you two-block this guy up."

Eason descended, and Greg Gibbons reeled the man up. Approximately one minute later, he pulled what appeared to be a corpse into the rear cabin.

"He's dead, sir," Gibbons radioed. "He's not breathing. He's still smoking."

"Smoking?" Eason thought, as he rose to a safer altitude. "But there wasn't any fire."

Eason turned and glanced over his shoulder at the man riding the rescue basket. It was something he wished he hadn't done, because from his viewpoint the man, with his neck bent backwards at a ninety-degree angle, appeared to have been decapitated. The hoisting cable had inadvertently formed a noose around his neck and wrapped itself around the basket, too, creating a tangle of cable, basket, and flesh.

"We hung him," recalls Eason. "There's no question about it. That's how we brought him up."

Luckily, Dias' backside had, by chance, come to rest on the edge of the basket. This offset just enough of his body weight, as he dangled from a twisted loop in the cable, to prevent his neck from snapping. Even so, the man was not breathing. He'd been coated in repeated dousings of jet fuel and perhaps the first trickle of the several hundred thousand gallons of bunker fuel that would soon wash ashore. As a result, the dark-skinned crewman from India did, indeed, look like someone who'd been charred by fire.

Regardless of Dias' appearance and condition, Gibbons disentangled him and pulled him aboard. Dave Neel, Brian Lickfield, and Doug Watson helped roll the corpse on its side, and worked to clear the man's mouth of grease and debris—just in case, somehow, he wasn't actually dead.

"Greg, get the basket ready," said Tim Eason finally. "And I'll attempt to locate some more survivors."

All at once, after the helicopter had first crashed, Eason had spotted the heads of five live ones who had somehow managed to escape the cramped confines of its interior. But the fifth one had now vanished from sight.

Eason, Kornexl, and Gibbons returned to the search then, screening the transitory arena of surf speeding past inside the twin circles of the H-65's individually controlled (one to a pilot) searchlights projecting out from under the copter's belly.

Ever conscious of the waves slamming into the cliffs nearby, and the threatening fountains of sea spray erupting off the *Selendang Ayu*, Eason battled back and forth across the frenzied waters just off the freighter's stern.

He, Kornexl, and Gibbons scrutinized every inch of the sea for more survivors. Still, faced with the sudden and unpredictable slap of roving wind cells, the last thing Eason wanted to do was to save four people, "only to lose them again by crashing into those cliffs."

With little fuel remaining, and a full cabin in back, Eason and Kornexl decided to fly over to the *Alex Haley* and lower the three survivors and one lifeless sailor onto the cutter's launch pad. They had hoped to refuel the H-65 in midair and then rush back and continue the search. Transitioning to forward flight, Eason left the island of light behind, and flew out into the darkness in the general direction of the *Alex Haley*.

"Coast Guard cutter *Alex Haley*, this is rescue 6513," radioed Rob Kornexl. "Request that you set flight-con-one for recovery of helo."

"Negative!" came the curt reply. "We are not within limits. We are unable to recover the helo at this time."

"Negative," countered Rob Kornexl, equally dogmatic, for he was certain that if, by some miracle, more survivors were still alive in the water at that moment, they'd be 100 percent dead by the time they were able to fly the H-65 to Dutch Harbor, refuel it, and make it back again. Offloading those they now carried onto the *Alex Haley* would allow them to return to the search almost immediately.

"This is 6513," Kornexl reinterated. "We are coming

in to off-load. Request that you set flight-con-one to recover the helo."

There was a pregnant pause, a thirty-second gap in which all communications ceased.

Rob Kornexl could only imagine what was going through Cdr. Bell's mind at that moment. "Something like 'Good God! I cannot even *believe* they're going to try and off-load those guys in this darkness in such extreme seas!'"

"Roger," came the eventual response from the *Alex Haley*. "Will have flight-con-one set in approximately ten minutes."

As they closed on the *Alex Haley*, those riding in back felt less than enthusiastic about the idea. In fact, when they caught sight of the postage stamp–sized landing area lit up and surrounded by an unpredictable ocean, bouncing around in the darkness below like a Mexican jumping bean, they were quick to share their concerns.

"Oh, please God," ran the sentiment of the survivors. "Don't try to put us down on that!"

It was then, recalls Tim Eason, that the voice of his flight mech cut in over the ICS intercom system.

"Hey, this guy just took a breath!" announced Gibbons, his voice filled with incredulity. He paused to evaluate the man further. "Sir, this man is in critical condition. He needs more medical help than anyone on the *Alex Haley* can give him. We really need to deliver this guy to the medical clinic they have in Dutch Harbor."

Quickly reassessing the situation, Eason radioed the *Alex Haley*. "Never mind," he said. "We are departing scene and heading to Dutch Harbor."

Rob Kornexl was relieved to hear the news as well, although he experienced a fleeting sense of guilt over his own reticence at not wanting to deliver to the cutter. Yet, when the idea was finally canceled, and he realized they no longer had to perform the off-loading maneuver in such nightmarish circumstances, he viewed it as a "wonderful thing."

As chief navigator aboard the H-65, Kornexl checked the GPS, correlated that information onto his charts, and quickly confirmed their position. Then he inserted a number of designated waypoints on the computer so they might find their way around the island "without sideswiping any volcanoes."

Eason asked Gibbons if he could reach their night-vision goggles. In the tight space of the aircraft's rear cabin, the flight mech managed to locate only one set, and passed that headgear forward into the cockpit.

"Give them to Rob," said Eason, "so he can fly us back."

Donning the NVGs, Rob Kornexl took over the controls. Several times as they journeyed along, snow squalls conspired to block the passage. Some were so filled with precipitation that they appeared as a solid green mass on their radar screen. Kornexl was fairly certain that they were over open water, but crabbing sideways as they traveled, with their radar pointed askew and wind gusts jolting them left and right, the overall experience was unsettling.

Also of grave concern was the problem of icing. Unlike the H-60 Jayhawk, their H-65 had no deicing capabilities built into her rotor blades. Carrying a maximum load of crew and survivors, as they were, they'd need all the lift they could summon. To avoid the heavy icing conditions that awaited them above three hundred feet, Kornexl chose to fly at the relatively low altitude of just one hundred and fifty feet above the sea.

The trip back to Dutch turned out to be one of the bumpiest rides both Kornexl and Eason had ever experienced. They "just got hammered!" They encountered headwinds so extreme that, although their airspeed read 180 knots (200 mph), they were actually moving ahead at just 80 knots (92 mph). Still, Kornexl kept the power maxed out anyway, because it was crucial that they get the injured man help as soon as possible.

"How is everybody back there, Greg?" Eason inquired.

"Everybody is wet and covered in oil, sir," replied Gibbons. "Otherwise they're all right. Except for the one guy who came up unconscious. But he's breathing now, and appears to be hanging in there."

While enroute, Tim Eason was able to establish radio

contact with USCG District 17 headquarters back in Juneau. He informed them that they needed to coordinate with the arrival of their H-65 in Dutch Harbor. "We're going to need to have an ambulance waiting for us," he said. "We have a man on board here who's severely hypothermic."

As they pounded their way through the jolting bursts of arctic air, Tim Eason could not help but feel sorry for the survivors stacked in the rear cabin. When packing a full load, as they now were, the H-65 flew along with its nose tilted forward fairly sharply. From the perspective of the passengers in back, all they were able to see was the unsettling vision of whitecaps flashing through the aircraft's landing lights below, giving them the distinct impression that their new pilots were about to crash them into the sea all over again.

Eason's wife Mary Ann had probably already heard about the crash. News of such events spread through the military families like wildfire. Their daughter Samantha's fourth birthday was just next month. Eason bore an abiding love for his family, but he wasn't about to worry about that kind of thing in the middle of a mission. If history, experience, and years of hard training had taught aviators like him anything, it was to mentally compartmentalize one's personal life. He was certain that the best thing he could do now was focus on the task at hand.

TWELVE

For a time, as the H-65 sprinted toward Dutch, Dave
Neel felt better. It was a huge relief to have Doug Watson
and Brian Lickfield on board. Watson and his wife Col-
lene were dear friends of he and his wife Rose. The crewmen had been airlifted to safety not a second too soon.

He was also relieved to know that young Aaron Bean
had not been strapped into his body harness in the rear
cabin of their H-60 at the time of the crash, as he normally was. With seven other survivors wedged in all around
him, the odds of finding one's way out of the confines of
such a dark, inverted, flooding space, with a panicking
mob of disoriented sailors all trying desperately to escape,
were slim.

When things became a little overheated in the rear cabin, Neel asked co-pilot Rob Kornexl to turn the heater off. Neel was lying alongside the high-revving contraption when it shut down. The sound it produced, however, was quite similar to the whine the main engines on Neel's helicopter had made when they flamed out, and for a few heart-pounding seconds he was sure they were going down again.

Aaron Bean knew that, trapped as he and the captain were out on the open deck of a sinking ship in the Bering Sea, surviving the present predicament would be the challenge of a lifetime.

Once, after dodging the deck wash of yet another aggressive wave, he glanced up in time to see the rescue basket with one of the crash victims inside it, rising toward the H-65 hovering far overhead. It was a comforting vision and, to him, served notice that they were doing their job, and he was doing his.

In truth, Bean believed that the H-65 was probably their only hope. Yet due to the limited space on board the much smaller copter, he did not expect them to airlift him or the ship's captain on that particular sortie. So when the helicopter flew away, vanishing into the darkness and leaving them to fend for themselves, he understood completely. They had to go and take care of business, to do what needed to be done. His extensive training had prepared him, up to a point, to be left there behind enemy lines.

Cut off from help by the wind and sea, marooned in some primitive reach of the Aleutian Islands without his rescue swimmer's equipment, and with no backup whatsoever, Aaron Bean found himself teetering on the razor's edge of survival. Some of the waves stealing aboard now were "enormous! They would crash onto the third and fourth stories of the pilothouse, leaving it completely awash." Yet no matter how bad it got he was determined to look after the lone survivor in his care, and to remain in the game. He would face down his fears and do his best to deal with the extreme nature of the isolation and ferocious weather.

Then he received a radio call from the *Alex Haley*, informing him that they had retrieved all three air crewmen from the wreckage. However, off-loading onto the leaping flight deck of the cutter had apparently been ruled out. Someone on board the aircraft had been injured pretty badly and they'd been forced to leave Bean and Singh on the freighter for now, and rush the afflicted one, along with the other survivors, back to Dutch Harbor.

Bean was worried that his good friend Brian Lickfield, the flight mechanic on the H-60 when it crashed, may have been the one injured, but he stifled the impulse to radio the H-65 to confirm it because he knew in his heart that Tim Eason and his crew had it covered.

"Go ahead," he thought, urging them on in spirit. "Do whatever you have to do to save the guy's life, whoever he is."

The H-65 Dolphin helicopter and its crew were halfway to Dutch Harbor when the legs of the unconscious Dias suddenly started to kick. It began with a single, spasmodic thrust; others soon followed. "By the time we landed in Dutch," recalls Neel, the man was "almost drum-kicking me." Secretly, though, Neel felt that somehow he deserved it. "I wanted to bring all of your buddies back alive," he silently acknowledged. "So just keep kicking."

When they landed at Dutch Harbor, all the emergency vehicles and folks were there waiting for them, including an ambulance and police cars, their lights flashing. The immigration people were there, too, everything you'd expect to see in response to such a rescue effort after a crash.

The second the chopper landed, Gibbons slid the cabin door open, and the ambulance crew rushed forward. All they seemed to notice was Rajiv Dias, the lone survivor in this bunch from India. He was apparently kicking like hell, so they subdued him, lifted him onto the stretcher, tied him down, and rushed him into the ambulance. Then, with sirens blaring and lights ablaze, the local police and medical teams raced away, leaving the weary, fuel-covered Coast Guardsmen who'd swum out of the same copter crash behind, alone and unattended, on the airport's icy, wind-lashed runway.

Climbing down out of the H-65 Brian Lickfield saluted comrades Eason, Kornexl, and Gibbons, patting each one on the shoulder. "Thank you," he said. "I love you guys."

"There was not much else I could say," Lickfield added later. "They had to fuel up and go back and get Aaron Bean and save the ship's captain, who were still stranded out there on the bow of the *Selendang Ayu*. . . . I owe those guys my life," he continued sadly. "I mean I wouldn't even be here talking to you now, if they hadn't been able to do what they did."

Neel, Watson, and Lickfield eventually rode to the medical clinic in police cars. They gave blood and urine samples, and wrote out their statements.

Hiding from the elements in the lee of the bow, Aaron Bean had chosen a position with a fairly respectable view of the sea and his surroundings. The mastlights beaming out across the water from atop the wheelhouse of the stern half of the *Selendang Ayu* illuminated the peaks of the storm waves as they lumbered past.

"The seas were huge, black, and ferocious," says Bean. "It was mean. It was wild. We had not only swells, but a breaking surf riding on top of them."

As each new wave came powering out of the darkness, Bean would turn to the captain and shout, "Here it comes, sir! Hold on! Hold on!" Then wave water would come crashing onto the deck, often as not lapping all the way forward, and leaving the beleaguered pair standing waist deep in a breathtaking rush of frigid sea. Often, when the bow of the giant ship rose and the draining waters poured over her sides, she looked like a submarine rising from the depths.

Confronted with such formidable dangers, Aaron Bean began preparing to abandon ship. He wanted to avoid entering the water at all costs. But when the stern of the *Selendang Ayu* had run aground, she'd become a helpless target, and the mammoth waves slamming into her entire length seemed bent on destroying her.

If the *Selendang Ayu* were to roll onto her side, spilling Bean and the vessel's last remaining survivor into the sea, their one hope—should they survive the initial plunge into the rushing waters—would be to somehow reach the life raft. The odds of surviving the rampaging surf inside such a thin-skinned contraption without an engine, anchor, or paddles seemed incalculably small.

What good would paddles do, anyway, against surf waves slamming into the coast at better than thirty-five miles per hour? But there was always the outside chance that the raft carrying them could survive the ride into shore. There were some narrow strips of rock beach along the base of some of the cliffs. Besides, if the life raft could extend, even for a couple of minutes, the time the crew of the H-65 had to reach them, it would be worth the effort.

The life raft—probably an eight- or ten-man version, Bean suspected—had yet to be deployed. It was, in fact, still folded inside the bulky, white rectangular box that it came in. The box was about three feet square and five feet long. When Bean first spotted it, the life raft container was nestled snuggly in its cradle, fastened securely in place on the deck, not far from the original hoisting area.

For lack of any other viable options, the more Bean thought about the raft the more convinced he became that he needed to reach it. Understandably, given the circumstances, he wasn't looking forward to venturing out into such an exposed area of the deck to try to retrieve it.

The bow of the ship rocked violently as the tireless onslaught of storm waves plowed repeatedly into her midships. As before, sometimes these waves would catch the ship just right at the bottom of its roll and scoop up the oncoming seas; occasionally, wave water several stories high came powering aboard. Accelerating like a runaway avalanche as the pitching vessel rolled the other way, this frightening wall of water would come roaring down the deck, crashing over the top of the cargo holds and erupting against the bases of the tall steel crane towers.

Ignoring the risks, and refusing to wait any longer, Bean sprinted to the life raft box and attempted to yank it free. But it felt far too heavy for one man to lift alone. He was still struggling with it when another wave came crashing aboard, sweeping his legs out from under him. Halting his slide, Bean leapt to his feet, ran back to their fo'c'sle hideout, and paused there briefly to check on the captain and allow himself to shake off his exhaustion.

If he and the captain were going to survive at all, they would have to dodge the tsunami-sized storm waves now scouring the deck clean. Time it wrong and they stood a good chance of being crushed against one of the hatch covers, or carried along at breakneck speed and being virtually torn apart as they passed through the side railings awaiting them. Equally grim was the lonely oblivion of heart-stopping sea awaiting them, broken body or not, just over the side.

Without warning, the ship rolled, and another large wave came crashing aboard. It tore the life raft from its mount and sent it tumbling. During one of those rare moments of slack water on deck as the ship struggled to right herself, Bean spotted the box floating.

"It's not safe," he acknowledged. "I could easily get swept overboard." He paused to think it through. "Do I really have to go out there to get that life raft? Will it save us? Is it worth the risk?"

Now Aaron Bean thought of Joseph Ungerheier, a former rescue swimmer and a hero of his. Once during a rescue off Kodiak Island, Ungerheier had reportedly climbed aboard a sinking crab boat and managed to save a life when he lifted a refrigerator off an injured fisherman trapped beneath it. He was awarded an Air Medal for his trouble. It was, in good part, Ungerheier's cocky retelling of that very story that now inspired Bean to go out there after the life raft.

Bean was also aware that Joey "the Grizz" Gryzenia, part of Doug Cameron's crew who were presently grounded back in Cold Bay, had also been flying on-scene and performing vital rescues. Joey, he knew, was the essence of bravery and testosterone. He couldn't let Joey think he was less of a man than he was. Or Ungerheier, for that matter.

In 1985, the Coast Guard began their rescue swimmer program. Since then hundreds of lives have been saved by a stellar lineage of heroic young men who, like Ungerheier, managed to be there and put it all on the line when it mattered the most. Men such as Jeff Tunks, Joseph "Butch" Flythe, Mike Odom, Tony Trout, Tom Bohland, Bob Watson, John Hall, A. J. Thompson, Rich Sansone, Harold Honnald, Mike Fish, Wil Milam, and O'Brian Hollow are recognized today as being some of America's finest.

As an heir to the courageous way these fine rescue swimmers had faced their individual demons, Aaron Bean felt an innate sense of responsibilty. He knew that they could "swim fast and hard and long, and [that] they could run fast and hard and long." Well, he, too, would make an accounting of himself. On this night, by God, Aaron Bean would also step forward and make a difference.

"If I don't do anything else heroic tonight," he thought finally, "I'm going to step out there in between waves, and I am going to grab that line and pull that raft up the deck to us."

As he prepared to make his move, he felt more alert than at any time in his life. He had moved swiftly so far, making decisions quickly and decisively. Then he spied the raft's bowline being washed back and forth in the current, and he thought, "This is my chance!"

He told himself that should he survive the risky maneuver, he would always look back upon it as the "bravest moment" of his young life. Summoning all his courage, then, he dashed out across the open deck.

Grabbing the thin, 5/8-inch nylon line trailing along in the water, and watching for waves as he worked, he set his feet and began pulling. The raft refused to budge. Each time a new wave broke up and over the side, the bow section of the ship would roll heavily and the water would once again begin jetting down the slanting deck. But then, as it rolled back, the life raft container would sometimes float free. Hoping to time his efforts to coincide with this phenomena, Bean heaved mightily on the line. The life raft moved perceptively closer.

Each time, it seemed as the ship rolled back, the force of the deck wash speeding down the tilting slope of the deck would threaten to carry the life raft away, and then Bean would rush to tie off the line and wait for the next opportunity. Eventually exhausted from what looked to be a successful effort, Bean made a radio call to the *Alex Haley*.

"I've secured the life raft," he reported. "I'm hanging in there, but I'm prepared to abandon ship if necessary."

The advice from command central was straightforward: He was to remain on the ship as long as possible.

Minutes later, Bean spied more slack in the cord leading to the life raft. Leaping into action, he rushed to gather all he could. When the deck shifted once again, and waist-deep wave water went roaring down it, Bean did his best to keep the life raft from being swept away. Though the force of it was almost too much for him, he did manage to slow the speed of the line slipping out through his hands and keep it from breaking.

Then another oversized breaker washed aboard, flooding the area. When the line leading to the life raft grew slack once more, Bean again seized his chance. The raft was apparently floating, and he began pulling in the line as fast as his hands could fly. As the loose coils fell at his feet, Bean's hopes rose. Should the ship sink from under them before the H-65 got back from Dutch Harbor, he and Captain Singh now had a better chance of surviving it.

While the telltale weightlessness of the last few feet of line slipping toward him through the water served to inspire him, the unexpected arrival of the stub end of it, now severed, caught him by surprise. The last massive storm wave had evidently swept up the bulky life raft container, carried it down the full 114-foot width of the deck, and launched it over the side, never to be seen again.

Deeply disappointed, Aaron Bean radioed the news to command center.

"Alex Haley! Alex Haley!" he said. "This is rescue swimmer 6020. Rescue swimmer 6020. Please be informed, I have lost the life raft. Over."

"Roger. Good copy. You have lost the life raft."

In spite of everything, Aaron Bean continued to dote on the last survivor under his care. When Singh's fingers became too numb from the cold dunkings to tie the laces of the street shoes he wore—laces that had become undone in all the commotion—he asked Bean to assist him. The rescue swimmer was glad to help.

Taking off his own soaked cotton flight gloves, he knelt to the task. But by the time he'd finished his hands had become so cold he couldn't get his gloves back on. So he stuffed the soaking-wet ones into his pockets and pulled out a pair of high-quality neoprene gloves that he'd been saving. They were waterproof, insulated, heavy duty, and comfortable, with individual fingers that allowed him to grip things and do his work. Snug inside them, Bean's hands eventually began to warm again.

Later, Bean overheard the radioman on the *Alex Haley* call for another helicopter. The rescue swimmer longed to see another plane arrive on-scene. But Air Station Kodiak was nearly five hundred miles away. Any helicopter still sitting on the ground in Kodiak wasn't going to do anyone any good on this night. By the time copter and crew arrived on-scene, one way or another the life-and-death drama currently playing out would be over.

When the H-65 headed toward Dutch Harbor with four survivors, Cdr. Matt Bell and his staff in the wheelhouse of the *Alex Haley* were left to struggle with one principal problem: How to get Aaron Bean and his ward off the foundering ship safely?

One of Cdr. Bell's fearless bosun's mates soon appeared in the wheelhouse with the answer. He wanted to launch the cutter's RHI (Rigid Hull Inflatable) raft over the side, and motor over to the freighter to rescue the men.

"We'll go over there and get them," he said.

"Hey, we don't launch an RHI in thirty-five-foot seas," Cdr. Bell countered. "I'm sorry."

"But sir, we think we can get the RHI in the water and get safely away from the ship."

"Look, you're absolutely right," replied Cdr. Bell. "In this boat, we ride low enough; you could probably launch the boat. But I couldn't recover you! You'd go riding the top of a wave and end up on our flight deck, as rough as it is out. And once you get all your people in the small boat, what are you going to do with them? Come alongside and have them shimmy up our Jacob's ladder? We have a tough enough time doing that in just eight-foot seas!"

During the night, as he waited for the H-65 to return, Aaron Bean allowed himself to drift emotionally for a few minutes and to wind down. But he quickly countered that notion.

"This is definitely not a time to relax," he thought. "You need to keep your guard up. Your senses must remain sharp. Don't you be letting your guard down now. Not for a moment. Not until this whole thing is over."

Bean felt himself moving back into his game, then. He took a deep breath, set his jaw, and noticed the muscle tension returning as he drew closer, once again, to the emotional edge he judged necessary to remain in the moment, and carry on.

THIRTEEN

With the wheelhouse lights dimmed down now, the *Alex Haley* idled ahead. Cdr. Bell could see the soft amber glow of the instrument panel reflecting off the torso of the navigator, who was plotting their course and position.

"Now it's completely black outside," he recalls, "and we're riding out this storm, and all you can hear is just the waves, and the wind, and the ship pounding." The waves were much larger than they were before. "Every fourth or fifth wave was coming up to our bridge windows," thirty-six feet above the vessel's flat waterline.

There was also some problem in the communications with Aaron Bean. Due to no fault of his own, the quality of his radio messages echoing inside the wheelhouse of the *Alex Haley* were often difficult to understand. Standing out on the open deck of the *Selendang Ayu*, engulfed in a kind of climatic hell, many of his dispatches going out over his small, handheld radio were indecipherable.

"Look," said Cdr. Bell, speaking aloud to Lcdr. Thorne and everyone on watch in the wheelhouse, "our one and only goal right now is to reassure Petty Officer Bean that we're doing all that we can to get him."

The officers and crew quickly agreed that any time they spoke to Bean on the radio, they would make every effort to talk to the young man in a personal, heartfelt, and encouraging way. Their questions would be kept short and simple, their conversations carried out in a calm, optimistic tone.

"But how," Cdr. Bell asked himself, "can I personally convey a sense of reassurance to this young rescue swimmer who's so suddenly been handed such awesome responsibilities?"

Finally, Cdr. Bell took hold of the radio mic and keyed it.

"Petty Officer Bean," he began, "this is Commander Bell, the captain of the *Alex Haley*. I just want to assure you, Aaron, that the calls you've made to us have been heard. Our helicopter crew has picked up some survivors and is presently flying them to Dutch Harbor." Bell also added that he had a son about Aaron's age, a Marine who was serving in Iraq, and that he would no more abandon the young petty officer in his predicament than he would a member of his own family.

"Aaron, we're working hard to get you back," Bell added. "The helicopter is going to return, and we're going to bring you back safely. Your whole charge now is to make sure that the master there is all right." Bell paused. "So how is the skipper? How's he holding up? Is he warm enough? Does he have a coat? Have you found a safe place for him to stand?"

"*Alex Haley*, this is Petty Officer Bean. Yes, sir. I believe I have."

He was pleased by the young rescue swimmer's response. "He took right to that," Cdr. Bell notes. "All his answers were spot-on professional." As the conversation progressed, Bell and the others standing in the *Alex Haley*'s wheelhouse came to the same conclusion: Aaron Bean sounded solid.

Cdr. Bell also suggested that since the H-65 would soon be returning, Bean and the captain might consider making their way to the stern of the vessel to the pilothouse, because that would probably allow them a better angle from which to hoist.

"No, sir," replied Bean. "I think we're going to stay right here."

Aaron Bean was touched by the commander's encouraging call. It was an incredibly decent thing for him to do.

"Roger, *Alex Haley*," he added. "This is rescue swimmer from the 6020. Good copy. I will contact you on a ten-minute coms schedule. Over."

"He's got it!" Cdr. Bell announced, pleased at the young man's response. "Now all we need is a helicopter to return and we can finish this mission!"

Then, without warning, all communications with the shipbound rescue swimmer ceased. Twenty minutes passed with no further word. Those on board the *Alex Haley* worked feverishly to reestablish radio contact. But nothing.

Unbeknownst to all, the *Selendang Ayu*'s hull had been punctured as it drifted into the rocky shallows of Unalaska Island. Then, as the wind and seas pushed the ship farther aground, several of her giant cargo holds had begun to fill with salt water.

The first that Aaron Bean unequivocally knew of it was when air began issuing from a series of shoulder-high vent pipes. These five-inch pipes rose from the deck in the shape of the curved end of a candy cane. Water was apparently rising so fast inside several of her holds that the velocity of the displaced air being forced out through them began producing a hissing sound.

With the vessel's stern now hard aground, and her free-floating bow rising and falling through an endless barrage of oncoming waves, more holes were being punched in her hull. As more cargo holds became compromised and sea-water rose inside the ship, and the unimaginable tonnage of those waters came to bear fully upon her, the *Selendang Ayu* started to settle into the sea. As it sank, the pressure of es-caping air rose to a kind of haunting groan, like storm winds moaning through a ship's rigging.

Soon, vent pipes up and down the deck were issuing similar sounds. Eventually, seawater came pouring out of them. When Captain Singh saw this, his face wore a look of extreme apprehension. The young rescue swim-mer could see that he was clearly unnerved, because he knew very well that the holds were flooding and that his ship was sinking.

Studying the world around him, then, Aaron Bean was dumbfounded by what he saw. Some five hundred feet away stood the enormous steel face of the wheel-house. It was as tall and wide as a six-story apartment building, with radar and masthead rising several stories above that, and it appeared to be leaning forward out over the deck in front of it. It was so strange. The giant, one-hundred-foot-wide wheelhouse continued to tilt farther and farther forward, and as it did the bow they were stand-ing upon also began to rear up. For some inexplicable rea-son, the *Selendang Ayu* appeared to be warping itself into the shape of a soup bowl.

Soon, Bean and Singh were alerted by the catastrophic sounds of hull failure reverberating through the deck underfoot. Then something similar to a sonic boom shook the night.

Bean looked at the captain.

"What was that?" he asked.

"The ship! It's breaking!" he replied.

Next, experiencing a total structural failure, the tension and power that had come to bear on both ends of the vessel seemed to suddenly release, and the stern and bow portions of the ship rocked back on themselves in the water. Then, as if in slow motion, the entire front half of the *Selendang Ayu*'s deck started to break away, splitting in two at the very center of the vessel, in the middle of the fourth hold. The entire front half of the ship, approximately three hundred feet—including two sixty-foot-high cargo cranes, deck, bow, fo'c'sle, and foremast—began to drift away.

Aaron Bean was astonished by the sudden turn of events. The whole thing seemed so surreal. For not unlike the fateful finish of the *Titanic* herself, the force of the sea had taken the giant, man-made monstrosity of the *Selendang Ayu* and broken her back, snapping her in two like a twig.

Strangely, however, the ensuing moments of the actual parting were not noisy at all. As the two unwieldy halves of the huge ship drifted apart, Bean saw exposed wires smoking and sparking. Then the bow section carrying him and the captain began to swing around, pivoting on the one remaining anchor.

Cut off from the stern section of the ship floating a thousand or so feet in the distance, Bean and the captain stood silently surveying the scene. Almost identical in length to the section now carrying them, the stern half of the ship pivoted briefly, and then was driven farther aground onto the same reef at the very edge of the surf zone. Some of her generators must have continued to produce electricity, however, because on that December night, she remained lit up like a Christmas tree.

The mastlights shining out from atop her wheelhouse in the distance illuminated every detail of the bizarre-looking stub of her foredeck and the peaks of the world-class storm waves rolling in from the Bering Sea. The ridges at the very tops of some of the waves were shot through with the crisp white light beaming across the water, while the broad shadows of wave troughs, some several hundred feet wide, advanced across the moody face of the sea.

It was a relief, however, to be out of the glaring scrutiny of those same mastlights and away from the ceaseless, unnerving sounds of the ship's alarms blaring.

Bean turned to Captain Singh.

"Why aren't we sinking?"

The captain explained with hand gestures and in his

broken English that their half of the ship must still have had sufficient air trapped in her many compartments to remain afloat.

The question now was, how long would that last?

Those in the wheelhouse of the *Alex Haley* were worried. They "kept calling, and kept calling, and kept calling," recalls Matt Bell. But they heard only silence.

"There was myself," says Cdr. Bell, "the X/O, the OD, a helmsman, the bosun's mate of the watch, and the quartermaster of the watch. And everyone's kind of got their necks cricked, listening to the radio, while trying to do their jobs at the same time."

It was quiet. The glow of amber light emanating off the energized surfaces of numerous instrument control panels bathed the interior of the bridge in soft hues of roseate red. A slight buzzing sound surged from the powerful GSB 9000 radio in the corner. Those present could also detect the rhythmic rocking of the floor underfoot hesitating, now and then, as the *Alex Haley* staggered under the muscular impact and leaden burden of yet another formidable storm wave.

Then, suddenly, a static-filled radio message from Aaron Bean cut through the tense silence of the cutter's wheelhouse.

"*Alex Haley! Alex Haley!* This is Petty Officer Bean!"

"Dude, where'd you go? You had us worried," shot back Cdr. Bell.

"Well, sir, it's like this," Cdr. Bell recalls a very cool Aaron Bean saying. "We had to go and try to find a better place to stand. Because I think this ship has just broken in half."

Soon after that, the bosun's mate and his brave band of skiff-mates once again appeared on the bridge of the *Alex Haley*, raring to go. One of their own was stuck on board the freighter. He was just waiting there, along with the ship's master.

"Sir, let us go. Let us go," the bosun's mate said.

"Okay, now, just think for a minute," said Cdr. Bell. "I wouldn't let you go during the daylight hours, and now that it's dark outside, and the winds and seas are worse than ever, you think I'm going to give in? So what are you going to do?"

"Well, we've still got people there on the ship. We're going to go get them."

"But just how do you plan to go about doing that?" pressed Cdr. Bell. "They're up there fifty feet above the water. How are you going to reach them? What are they going to do? Jump?"

The gutsy Coastie assured Cdr. Bell that they would somehow make it happen.

"Yeah, right. Bean's going to take the ship's captain and jump fifty feet into the water, and then try to climb into the life raft in a rolling surf." Bell paused only briefly. "Forget it."

With the life raft gone, half the ship missing, and no helicopter in sight, Aaron Bean decided that, should the deck under his feet eventually sink entirely, he would grab the captain and drag him clear of the wreckage. After that he'd do his best, using his "survival swim," to keep the man afloat as long as possible. But he remained convinced that without his dry suit and gear, neither of them would last for long.

The lifeless bodies of shipwrecked victims killed in surf zones packing but a fraction of the unyielding force this one bore, were often pulled from the water with every stitch of clothing stripped away, and all body hair rubbed off, rendering them completely bald.

Remarkable as it may seem, from time to time, as he waited for his aviating brothers to return—and when he wasn't busy taking care of the captain "to make sure he didn't just up and float away"—Aaron Bean was able to transcend the siegelike nature of his circumstances, set aside his fears, and inhale the breathtaking panorama of the strange and unforgiving world that surrounded him. Sometimes, the stinging spatter of spray and ice would ease momentarily and the black cloud cover overhead would part, and then Aaron could make out the patterns of the stars, flawless and glittering in the heavens above.

Some who were there that night would recall brief intervals when it was "moon bright," but meteorologists researching that time and place claim that there was no such moon showing in that part of the hemisphere.

Once, after another fierce flurry of blizzard snow had blown through, the luminous, silvery light created by the mastlight beams revealed a sprawling white surf racing ahead on its final approach into Unalaska Island. In the clean, crisp air, the broad, treacherous spectacle appeared almost microscopic in detail, with wind-whipped tendrils of mist trailing off the far-flung breakers, and the intimidating, still-life vision of volcanic terrain rising up in all its savage splendor.

Aaron Bean found that the captain, by now, "was kind of like a puppy, you know. Like right by my side. He listened to everything I told him. He agreed to everything that I said. He was scared, and wet, and cold; he was just freezing!"

Referring to the starboard side upon which they were now making their stand, Captain Singh implored him,

"Have them, when they come back, come back on this side. THIS side!"

The young rescue swimmer could sense the captain's fear, and he did his best to reassure him.

Acknowledging the urgency of the moment, and the necessity of making a quick turnaround in Dutch Harbor, Tim Eason and Rob Kornexl had briefly entertained the idea of "hot-gassing" the H-65 (refueling it while on the ground, but with her jet engines running and her rotor blades still spinning). But Greg Gibbons' dry suit was covered in oil and jet fuel, as was Neel's, Watson's, Lickfield's, and Dias', the garroted survivor from India. Finally, with the aircraft's interior also coated, and blustery winds blasting the runway and fueling depot, they decided the smart thing to do was just shut the engines down and fill their tanks as quickly as possible.

The ambulance had already departed when one of the airport linemen came running out. "Hey!" he yelled. "There's an important phone call from the base back in Kodiak! It's for anybody who can take it!"

At the time, Greg Gibbons was busy refueling the H-65, and Rob Kornexl was working diligently to lay out their new flight plan, creating "solid lats and longs" to lead them back to the scene, so Eason ran into the hangar and picked up the receiver. Cdr. Phillips, the operations boss at Air Station Kodiak, was on the line.

"Are you guys all right?" he asked.

"Yes," Eason assured him, before giving a quick summary of the mission. Phillips wanted to make sure that, given what they had seen and all that had already happened out there, they were still okay to go back out.

"We're good to go," Eason assured him.

By the time he returned to the H-65, its refueling had already been completed. Standing out on the tarmac, then, Eason put it straight to Kornexl and Gibbons.

"I talked with the Air Station, and they say we're good to go if we want."

"Let's go get 'em!" said Greg Gibbons.

Rob Kornexl seconded the motion.

Tim Eason climbed inside the cockpit, strapped himself into his seat alongside Kornexl, and started the aircraft. He quickly discovered, however, that the pitot tubes—the instruments mounted on the nose of the helicopter and used to determine airspeed—had frozen shut. If those weren't operating correctly, he knew, it would render their flight director and the other systems on board their copter useless, and make navigating on such an inhospitable night virtually impossible. On top of that, their GPS was no longer tracking any satellites, leaving no way to vector their ever-changing positions as they traveled.

None of this was good news. The snow was being whipped up to a point where from moment to moment they could hardly see at all. Eason and Kornexl exchanged a look acknowledging the apparently unavoidable challenges that now lay ahead—one that seemed to say, "Well, that's just the way it is. So here we go anyway!"

With two people still out there, shipwrecked and in imminent danger, they taxied out across the ramp to position themselves for takeoff. Luckily, just as Eason was pulling pitch to take off, the aircraft's pitot tubes opened back up, and the GPS system came back online, restoring their navigation systems. It was a fortuitous turn of events, a timely bit of luck, because at that point both pilots were starting to have second thoughts.

Just the same, when Eason crawled into the sky and nosed ahead, picking his way over the steep, barren landscape that surrounds Dutch Harbor, he had less than two hundred feet of visibility in front of him. Flying along on such a night wearing night-vision goggles gave Kornexl and Eason a solid edge against the interminable darkness. When their vision was not obstructed by snow, they "could actually see pretty decently," says Kornexl. "It wasn't 20/20 vision; it was more like 20/40 acuity, but it was a huge plus over flying without them."

In their urgent desire to reach the *Selendang Ayu* before it rolled over and sank, Eason and Kornexl did their best to lay down the miles. Kornexl had prepared a solid flight plan to guide them back. Even so, they got jack-hammered from the outset. Each time they encountered yet another snow squall, the red glow of their anticollision instrument light would begin flashing and they felt compelled to slow down.

Technologically advanced as NVGs are, they have one significant disadvantage—the narrow, myopic view they offer. Wearing them is like peering out at the world through the tunnel-like radius of a soda straw. Now, as they battled their way ahead through the cold midair blasts, both pilots began experiencing brief bouts of vertigo as countless scattering snowflakes converged on them, reflecting back, as they flashed through their line of vision, like neon-green tracer bullets shooting past them in the night.

At one point while enroute, they received a clear radio transmission. The message was from the *Alex Haley* asking them to expedite their return, as the situation on-scene was presently deteriorating. No further explanation was given. Kornexl and Eason found it a rather strange message, considering that an H-60 helicopter had already crashed there, causing the deaths of at least six sailors, and that the *Selendang Ayu* was already hard aground when they left. How much worse, the pilots were left to wonder, could things have gotten?

FOURTEEN

Tim Eason and Rob Kornexl swung out from behind Makushin volcano on the backside of Unalaska Island and headed into Skan Bay to find the entire area veiled in darkness. The freighter's distinctive mastlights could no longer be seen. Perhaps the ship had gone to the bottom in their absence. If so, where were Aaron Bean and his charge?

Investigating further, what they saw proved confusing. In the reflective glow of their two small but intense searchlights, they soon came upon the giant, white figure of the *Selendang Ayu*'s wheelhouse. Her generators had finally given out. With her anchor in tow, the wind and seas had driven the ship sideways onto a hull-crunching mound of boulders.

Then, oddly, in the distance they spotted what looked to be the flash of Aaron Bean's strobe light. The intense, bluish-white flicker, however, was coming from a position that lay completely contrary to where one might expect. It looked to be perhaps five hundred feet away, yet it was suspended off in the black of night, and not at all aligned with the lay of the vessel. It was hard to figure.

As they flew nearer, Eason and his crew were stunned by what they saw. The storm had finally won out. In their absence, the unrelenting barrage of incoming breakers had taken the giant freighter and broken her in two. Those huge, individual sections since drifted apart. With their searchlights illuminating the amazing sight, Eason and Kornexl moved in for a closer look.

The storm winds had increased dramatically since they'd last been on scene. Surging winds of fifty to sixty knots were now raking the area, with individual williwaw gusts sprinting down off the nearby slopes of Makushin volcano and across the water at no less than seventy-five knots (85 mph). Undeterred by the horrific conditions, the intrepid crew of the H-65 pressed on.

Edging closer, they studied how far the leaping, wave-washed bow section had moved. Her anchor chain slanted steeply down from the starboard side of her bow and disappeared into the churning waters at the edge of the surf.

Then, Eason and Kornexl spotted Aaron Bean and the ship's captain huddled together. They'd found shelter from the storm as before, just aft of the fo'c'sle. But this time, they had done so on the starboard side.

The anchor and chain seemed to be keeping the giant piece of flotsam they were now riding from drifting any farther ashore. But it was clear that this portion of the ship was now sinking, and was being swatted back and forth by the building waves. Each time the point of her leaping bow would plunge into the new, oncoming surge, a virtual tidal wave of seawater would come crashing aboard, rolling over the top of her bow, and down over the hapless duo.

Trapped then on the front half of the *Selendang Ayu*, Bean and the captain could be seen struggling to keep their feet as they rode the chunk of junk now sinking beneath them. For Tim Eason, the sight of the minuscule forms of the two beleaguered castaways trying to keep from getting washed away as they rode the truncated bow section "over the waves at night," was an image that would remain with him always.

"So this is what they meant by 'deteriorated,'" put in Rob Kornexl.

In the darkness, Aaron Bean dropped his handheld radio. He was determined to find it before the next wave washed it away. He'd no sooner dropped it onto the unlit, sea-slickened deck at his feet when he heard the sound of someone radioing him. It was the voice of Tim Eason on board the H-65. Bless their hearts. Eason and his crew had finally returned for them.

"Coast Guard rescue swimmer! Coast Guard rescue swimmer! This is Coast Guard 6513!" radioed Eason.

Bean could hear him calling, but with his helmet on he couldn't pinpoint the radio's exact location. He searched the deck in the immediate area.

"Where is it anyway? Where is it?" he called out.

Then, chancing upon the radio, he was finally able to return the call.

"6513! 6513! This is Coast Guard rescue swimmer Aaron Bean!" he called out. "This is Bean from Cape May!"

Tim Eason was relieved to hear the sound of Aaron Bean's positive, energetic voice—certain confirmation that in their absence he'd managed to remain in the game.

Bean reiterated that he wanted his brothers in the air to bring a quick end to what had been a truly precarious ride.

"All right, Bean," interjected Eason. "We're going to come in at a fairly high hover."

"That sounds mighty fine to me, sir!" replied Bean, enthusiastically.

■   ■   ■

Erratic winds or not, Tim Eason wasted no time in maneuvering the H-65 into a hover position several hundred feet above the storm-tossed bow of the dismembered freighter. Facing offshore then, he pointed the chopper's nose directly into the wind.

"Rescue checklist, part two," he said.

The winds were blowing so intensely at that point, driving intermittent flurries of blizzard snow through the area, that the wave strikes impacting along the exposed sides of the freighter were regularly launching water spouts that shot eighty to one hundred feet into the air. With the destructive force of the exploding wave phenomena they had witnessed still fresh in their minds, Eason and Kornexl were understandably a bit gun-shy.

It was clear to both pilots that if Aaron Bean hadn't taken the ship's captain and relocated to the starboard side of the *Selendang Ayu* when he did, they'd have been chilled by the repeated drenchings into a catatonic state of hypothermia, or swept away altogether by now.

Given the direction of the wind and the shifting state of the bow, hoisting the pair from their new position presented several new and formidable aviation challenges. The worst impediments the pilots faced were the two huge, steel deck cranes, which were still standing. Rising

approximately sixty feet above the holds, and at least
ninety feet above the sea, each stanchion had an equally
large boom arm that extended out horizontally over the
deck. Rigging cables swooped down from the tops of these
cranes to the far end of those boom arms, like those on a
suspension bridge, leaving Greg Gibbons with the task of
keeping their precious rescue basket, and the 210 feet of
cable attached to it, from fouling on any of a myriad of potential hang-ups and obstructions.

With the lifeline of his cable and basket slanting back
and down toward the two drenched and ragged men
waiting below, Eason was forced to fly well out in front of
the ship's bow. At times, in such intense winds, he found
himself navigating so far out ahead of it, with the basket
trailing far behind, that he felt as though he were navigating in a vacuum, suspended inside a massive black hole,
with no reference points at all left to aid him.

The problem with trying to hoist off either side of the
bow of the freighter was that each time Greg Gibbons
succeeded in maneuvering the basket anywhere near its
mark, the hoist cable would swing in perilously close to
the crosslike form of the forty-foot-tall steel bow mast,
and he would end up having to wave Eason off and start
all over again. With no way to replace either the cable
or the basket in midflight, should a snag-up occur, the
H-65 and its crew would be forced, once more, to aban-

don Aaron Bean and the severely hypothermic captain and race back to Dutch Harbor for repairs.

Flying blind then, Eason and Gibbons made four failed attempts to hoist from the bow. Each, recalls Eason, came dangerously close to "wrapping the cable up in the mast."

"Hey, I can see the back part of the ship," put in Kornexl, referring to the stern section of the *Selendang Ayu* taking a pounding in the distance. Apparently driven by battery power, some soft cabin lights shined through the tiny, square stateroom windows on the face of the wheelhouse. By using the lights as a reference, he figured that he might be able to give the hoisting a go.

"Let me give it a try from the left seat," Kornexl suggested.

"Roger that," shot back Eason. "You have the controls."

Rob Kornexl grabbed the cyclic (control) stick and made several more attempts from the left seat. But, due to the threat of entanglement, Eason waved both of those off. For a time, Kornexl could make out the faint outline of the *Selendang Ayu*'s wheelhouse in the distance. But each time he started to hover into a favorable position, another smothering snow squall would move through, completely erasing their only reference.

It was under these impossible conditions, as he hovered inside the wild inundations of blizzard snow, that

Rob Kornexl experienced a bit of vertigo. To counter this, he handed control of the aircraft back over to Eason. Standard procedure.

Anyone who has watched the original *Star Wars* movie may well remember the tracerlike effect of all those stars speeding by the instant one of their spaceships jumped to light-speed. To Tim Eason, with his night-vision goggles flipped down over his eyes, the snowflakes sprinting past outside "looked exactly like that, except they were green."

Eason attempted to slip back into hoisting position and make it happen. But the peak of the Alaskan storm was now pelting the area, and the winds that had made everything so difficult were "just howling," forcing him to abort each new attempt.

"We've got to get this," Eason told his crew, while thinking to himself, "because I don't know how much longer I can do this."

With her holds partially flooded, the bow of the *Selendang Ayu* rose and fell more sluggishly now, teetering from side to side like a drunken sailor. The onslaught of tall, breaking seas battered what remained of her bow, striking it first on one side, then the other. This sent Aaron Bean and the ship's last survivor running for cover. Far too often, exceptional waves at least thirty feet high came angling in and exploded over her port side, sending virtual tidal waves of cascading sea down on them.

When one such wave crashed into the ship and erupted skyward, Aaron Bean and Captain Singh sought protection in the lee of the starboard side of the fo'c'sle as best they could. Regardless, they got thoroughly drenched.

It was equally clear to those in the air that the ship's captain—cold, tired, and embattled as he was—would not be able to endure such a beating indefinitely. Flying blind, with no visual references whatsoever, Eason maneuvered the H-65 through the icy arctic blasts, staggering "left and right, and fore and aft." Forty angst-filled minutes of intense effort passed without having achieved any real measure of success.

At that moment, Rob Kornexl was kicking himself for not being able to come up with a way to "get those guys off the deck before they, too, were lost." Should the starboard anchor chain holding them so tentatively in place suddenly part, as its port-side twin had done, the bow section would most likely drift sideways into the waiting surf and roll onto her side.

Or it might sink stub end first into the waiting depths, and possibly end up standing vertically, with only the tip of her bow pointing skyward, with her fo'c'sle protruding from the sea. Then the pitiless, growling storm waves would come calling and sweep away the last of the ship's weather-beaten survivors, killing them for sure.

Sensing the futility of their efforts, Eason and Kornexl ultimately became convinced that they would never be able to achieve a hoist by hovering off the bow, under the present conditions.

Then Rob Kornexl hit on an idea. Risky as it might seem, if Aaron Bean could take the ship's captain and move farther aft, out onto the open deck they were marooned upon, it just might provide the kind of visual reference they'd been searching for. If Eason could remain on station long enough, while looking straight down on the deck, such a stunt might allow Greg Gibbons enough time to maneuver the basket in close enough for Aaron Bean to snag it.

Rob Kornexl made the call.

"Rescue swimmer," he began, "this is Coast Guard rescue helo 6513. We can't get the basket down to you on deck there because you guys are too far forward. Request that you move aft on the vessel so we can complete this hoist."

Since the *Selendang Ayu* had broken in two, and her mastlights had been snuffed out, Aaron Bean hadn't been able to see much of anything outside of his own small arena, which was only momentarily illuminated every few seconds by the small, blinking strobe light mounted on top of his helmet. But with the H-65's two small yet sufficient searchlights moving back and forth across the area, he could see a good deal better now, and the idea of dodging treacherous storm waves, some the size of semi-trailers sweeping sideways across the freighter's open deck, seemed like the height of insanity.

"Sir," replied Bean, in a sincere tone, "I don't want to do that."

"Aaron, you've got to move aft," shot back Rob Kornexl. "Or we're not going to be able to pick you up."

"Aaron," added Eason, "you're going to have to go as far aft of your present position on the starboard side there as you possibly can. We need some kind of a reference point. You've got to give us something to look at."

"Roger, sir. We'll move aft."

Dragging the cold-stiffened captain along behind him then, Bean set out on another treacherous task. Staying in the lee of the fifty-foot-long cargo hold covers, he made his way down the deck on the starboard side straight into the area where some of the worst wave strikes had been occurring.

Hurrying across the open, unprotected gaps between the cargo holds, the force-10 winds spit molecules of stinging spray into their faces. It was the peak hour, the apex of the storm, and the waters of the Bering Sea responded in kind. They slammed into the side of what remained of the dismembered freighter with a menacing ferocity. Bean and Singh hid as best they could in the lee of the cargo holds, while frightening breakers came tumbling across the deck and over the holds, completely drenching them.

In between dunkings, Bean continued to advance. With the captain in tow, he ventured forth as far as he dared. But he refused to go to the very edge of the severed deck and stare directly down into the void where the breakers were washing into the bowels of the ship—not only because it was so profoundly unsafe, but because it would have been "just too much." Nevertheless, Bean led them to within a few yards of the ragged edge where the deck had been torn apart.

As they stood there waiting, these adventurous souls, one clad in a Coast Guard jumpsuit, the other in street clothes, got thoroughly and repeatedly doused. The waves striking the port side would wash over the cargo holds and "rinse right down on top of our heads," says Bean.

Worst of all, the breakers now arriving were laced with heavy doses of JP-5 jet fuel. Though the ceaseless tempest of wind offered some respite from the nauseating smell, each time a wave buried them, Bean was forced to purse his lips together to keep the caustic, petroleum-laced salt water out of his mouth.

Standing upright and positioned at each corner of the hold covers were seven-foot-tall boltlike mechanisms. In the dark, it was impossible to define the exact construction of these steel devices, but each one had a "gigantic nut on top of it," and were apparently used, one to a corner, to secure the cargo hold covers. On this night, one of these corner bolts would assist in keeping this tired pair of water-logged seafarers from washing away.

Each time a wave came roaring down upon them, Aaron Bean would turn and hug the tall, metal, boltlike fastener. It was about the thickness of a telephone pole. And looping one arm around it, he would reach out and seize the captain by the front of his life preserver with his free hand, and pin him there against the backside of the cargo hold. Then he'd take a breath, duck his head, close his eyes, and brace himself for the latest dunking. Bean was determined not to let go, nor to allow the force of the assailing currents to tear the good captain from his grasp.

The threads of the bolt, however, turned out to be lubricated with the stickiest, nastiest grease imaginable. His hands were soon covered with it. His helmet and body, too, were also being coated with repeated dunkings of the JP-5 jet fuel. The smell of it would not go away. Yet Bean remained unmoved, steadfastly committed to serving both as guard and host to the mission's last remaining survivor.

"Hey, Aaron," Tim Eason once again radioed from the H-65 far overhead, "this is going to be another high hoist."

"That sounds good to me, sir!" replied Bean.

■   ■   ■

With the combined sounds of the crashing seas, the buf-
feting winds, and the H-65's twin engines bellowing
overhead, there was no way to detect when the next an-
nihilating breaker would come crashing aboard.

Some of the huge waves now passing over Aaron Bean
and the captain came rolling aboard the ship and across
the deck almost intact, submerging the clinging survivors
in as much as fifteen feet of icy, suffocating sea. Waiting for
it to pass while completely buried in the cold, dark currents "was tough."

In between dunkings Aaron Bean tried to brief the
captain. "Sir, you are going to go first!" he yelled. "When
you get inside the basket, sit on your hands! Don't try to
get out of the basket until they pull you out! Okay?"

With the two, sixty-foot-high columns of the ship's
deck cranes rocking back and forth, one on either side
of them, the act of hoisting promised to be a rough-and-
tumble affair and a formidable challenge. Anything could
happen.

Without warning, another storm wave crashed aboard.
Ten or so feet of churning sea came spilling over the hatch
cover beside them. Huddled in the lee of it, Bean and
Singh once again held their breaths as the icy surge came
cascading down upon them. Had Bean not had a tight and
protective grip on the captain, the man would have surely

been lost, carried away by the tsunami-like force of the runaway currents.

Shaking off their latest deluge, Aaron Bean turned to the sodden figure of the ship's captain and drew him close.

"Captain! Listen!" he yelled. "Now, one more time, just so you have it! They're going to boom you up to the helicopter! And when it's time, they're going to pull you inside the cabin and dump you out! So don't try to climb out until they grab you and tell you to! Okay?"

"Yes. Okay, okay," agreed the captain.

Clearly hypothermic, the middle-aged man was shaking violently. His wet black hair lay matted against his forehead. For a time, he just stood and stared at Bean.

"Can I bring my briefcase?" he asked, tiredly.

Bean felt compassion for the beleaguered captain. He studied the leather case in the man's hand. He wanted to just chuck it over the side, but the case was a relatively small one with apparently important documents inside. Perhaps money. Besides, he figured it would not significantly interfere with the hoist, or prove much of a bother topside.

"Yes," replied Bean, reluctantly.

Drenched, exhausted from their ordeal, the two men stood and awaited. Aaron Bean could see the H-65 fighting for position in the blustery winds far above. Suddenly, the rescue basket came by almost within reach, but he was unable to grab it and it whipped past, climbed sharply, and was gone.

Then, using yet another sleight of hand, Greg Gibbons dealt the vengeful storm gods another defeat when he managed to maneuver the rescue basket on its descent through the unpredictable elements, and set it down on deck remarkably close by. Aaron Bean grabbed the captain and immediately began dragging his cold, stiff ward across the deck in the hopes of intercepting the basket, but it danced away before they could reach it. Twice, Bean found himself "totally psyched out" by other promising efforts, only to have the basket go flittering off again across the sky.

The young rescue swimmer and the captain from India had been out on deck for nearly three and a half hours now. With the thundering report of each new storm wave crashing aboard came the renewed fear of being cut off from the comparative safety of the fo'c'sle area they'd just abandoned. Bean could see that the ship's captain was becoming dangerously hypothermic. If the dunkings continued unabated, and the efforts of those trying to reach them from the H-65 overhead were to ultimately fail, the man would never live to see the dawn.

Aaron Bean seized Captain Singh and held on tight as another wave washed over them. He held his breath, accepted the dunking, then waited for the water to recede. As the flood of seawater bled away, the slightly built captain surfaced, coughing, his small dripping head bent forward in a pose of fatigue and resignation.

Reestablishing his footing, Bean breathed deep of the raw sea air. But when he looked up again, the sky was clogged with the countless, scattering particles of another blinding snowsquall, and the angelic vision of the H-65 and its crew who'd been battling so hard to reach them had vanished.

"That's just great!" announced Bean to no one. "Merry-by-God Christmas!"

Tired, chilled to the bone, Bean fought to keep his mind on the present moment, and to look after the captain.

"Be ready," he cautioned himself.

FIFTEEN

Pilot Tim Eason brought his H-65 in as low over the deck as he dared. Looking more or less straight down as he hovered in, the two tall steel deck cranes were swinging back and forth on either side of him like giant clubs ready, at the first misstep, to bat his copter out of the sky.

"Basket's going down," said Greg Gibbons.

Then he began giving conning commands. Most in-flight adjustments that flight mechs give their pilots are along the lines of "Back and right fifteen [feet]." But what Tim Eason heard was, "Back and right one hundred."

Eason listened intently, but without comment. Few pilots had ever heard such an exceptional conning request. The distance seemed impossibly far. Fantastic, even. Once this terrible night was over, it was something Eason hoped he'd never hear again.

Seated on the left side of the aircraft, Rob Kornexl served, in good part, as a lookout. But, just as Dave Neel had discovered, spotting the dark silhouettes of individual waves rolling out of the coal-black backdrop of night was an amazingly difficult feat. The speed and stealth with which they advanced was incredible.

Then with a familiar mastery, Gibbons once again defied the elements. He planted the rescue basket directly in front of Aaron Bean and his charge. As the cable whipped about overhead, Bean turned, grabbed the captain, and stuffed him inside, suitcase and all. "I had him sit on his hands," he recalls. "And then I reached my hand up as high as it would go, and gave those hovering above us the sharpest, clearest identification of a thumbs-up that I could."

Surfing the winds above, Tim Eason slid the chopper back until the angle of the hoist cable extending between the chopper and the basket was as close to straight up and down plum as he could get. Timing it perfectly, Gibbons made his move, yarding the captain off the deck at precisely the right moment.

Gibbons had just taken the load when, without warning, an invisible fist of wind slammed into the helicopter. Eason felt the H-65 leap out of position. He fought to regain station, but overcorrected and ended up giving both the basket and the captain inside it an "E-ticket ride." Eason pulled full collective and accelerated into the snow-filled heavens. Huddled inside the basket, dangling on the end of the cable, the captain had one wild ride, narrowly missing one of the tall steel stanchions.

Captain Singh rose toward the helicopter "like a bat out of hell," recalls Aaron Bean. The flight mech "took him up, up, and away! Quick and smooth. The basket made one big pendulum swing, and nearly smashed into one of those huge steel cranes that stand about sixty feet high in between the cargo holds . . . It was like nothing else. The basket was bright red and shining silver, with bright retro tape reflecting as it rose clear of the crane. It was a perfect sight."

And Bean thought, "Nice job, Gibbons! Good job!"

"I tell you, it was really something," recalls Bean. "I looked up at the sky, and the captain was on his way, and clear of the vessel. They swung him up there and boomed him into the cabin. The clouds had parted, and I could see the stars, and the mountains on the island close by. And I said to myself, 'This could be a good night after all.'" Bean "returned to holding onto the bolt." While he waited, another sneaker wave came crashing in over the top of him.

Minutes later, the rescue basket again glided in for its final landing. Swinging down, it bounced lightly once, then skidded to a stop alongside Bean. Applying an eagle's eye from his nestlike perch in the doorway of the H-65 overhead, and sailing definitively into the history books as one of the most gifted flight mechanics ever, Greg Gibbons had made yet another perfect drop. The basket had barely touched down when, quick as a cat, Aaron Bean leapt inside it.

Bean's heart was practically beating out of his chest as he assumed the position for the all-crucial ride at hand. And the boys overhead did not disappoint. It was a "huge hoist," and Gibbons brought his brave young subject up as fast as the block could go. It still proved to be quite a roller-coaster ride. And as he rose, Aaron Bean moved back and forth in broad pendulum swings, drifting through the wind-blown space for long seconds, before finally drawing near to the copter in ever-tightening circles.

As Aaron Bean closed on the H-65, Greg Gibbons stuck his boot out the copter's door. "This is something that generally only H-60 flight mechanics do," recalls Bean, approvingly. "By grabbing that boot, I could finally put a stop to all the swinging. Anyway, when I saw Gibbons do that, I reached out and grabbed his boot. I mean I embraced it! I knew what was going on. I, like, hugged his boot, and he boomed me into the cabin."

Popping out of the basket, Bean immediately hooked himself up to the aircraft's intercom system.

"Petty Officer Bean is on ICS, sir," he radioed, according to protocol.

"Bean! How are you doing?" asked Eason.

"I'm mighty fine, sir!" he replied.

Eason and Kornexl both turned around and gave Aaron Bean the thumbs-up.

"How do you feel?" Eason asked.

"Mighty fine, sir!" the rescue swimmer beamed.

"We're going to continue to search for survivors, now," Eason told him.

"Roger, sir!"

"We're going to use you as our rescue swimmer if we find anybody."

"That's fine, sir," replied Bean, still very much in the game.

Safely inside the rear cabin of the H-65, Aaron Bean refocused his attention on the care of the freighter's captain. The man was clearly hypothermic. His hands were so cold they were nearly frostbitten. Bean wrapped the shivering man in a wool blanket. Then he began placing small chunks of a Snickers candy bar in the man's mouth. Waiting patiently for him to finish chewing each piece, he held a small plastic bottle up to the captain's trembling lips, and assisted him in chasing each bite of the sugary snack by pouring half-swallows of fresh water into his mouth.

When he had finished, the drenched but grateful captain placed his trembling hands together in prayer fashion and, in accordance with the dictates of his Hindu religion, bowed respectfully.

"We got Aaron up, closed the door, and cranked the heat up," recalls Rob Kornexl, "because those guys were just freezing."

Leaving the wreckage of the *Selendang Ayu* then, the two pilots flew back and forth over the area just off the water, making "two very thorough, low-speed, low-altitude searches," adds Kornexl. "Both of the water leading out from the base of the cliffs, and along the shore."

"We have two landing hover lights," adds Tim Eason, "and they are individually controlled. There is a control for each light on each pilot's collective. Rob Kornexl is looking out his side of the aircraft and using his landing hover light, and I'm doing the same thing with mine on the right side of the aircraft."

They closely examined the surface of the sea as it swept past inside the bright, circular swaths of their lights. They had hoped to spot other survivors before they were sucked into the pulverizing thirty- and forty-foot breakers thundering ashore, or were totally annihilated on the craggy block of cliffs awaiting them, dead ahead.

They made several more sweeps of the shoreline, and were still searching when they went "bingo for fuel," which meant that they could no longer remain on-scene. "Also," adds Rob Kornexl, "we were pretty confident at that point that there was no one else left to save."

"*Alex Haley*, this is Coast Guard 6513," radioed Rob Kornexl. "We've conducted a thorough shoreline search. We have nobody in sight in the water, and nobody in sight on the shore. We are going to RTB [Return to Base] in Dutch Harbor and reassess."

"*Alex Haley*. 6513. Roger."

Reluctantly, then, they departed the scene.

For those standing by in the wheelhouse of the *Alex Haley*, the drama unfolding so perilously near to shore remained mostly an audio experience. When the H-65 first returned, Tim Eason radioed that he was hovering in to try to pick up Bean and the captain. "Then we heard nothing," recalls Cdr. Bell, "for what seemed like an eternity." Those standing in the wheelhouse experienced a "drop-dead silence."

Finally, Tim Eason reported that they had successfully recovered both Petty Officer Bean and the ship's captain, and had completed a thorough search of the shoreline and adjacent waters, as well.

"Okay, X/O!" barked Cdr. Matt Bell. "Give the ops boss a call. I want a course out of here! I don't care where we go, but I don't want to be anywhere near this bay tonight. We're gone!"

Inside the H-65's cabin, where the shivering survivors sat, the air reeked with the smell of jet fuel and bunker oil. The stainless-steel rescue basket, too, was solid black, covered in goo.

"Once we were done hoisting the guys from the crash site," recalls Tim Eason, "we headed southwest, away from the island, because we didn't have a flight plan to get us around the mountains yet. We were heading straight into the wind, and we had 140 knots [160 mph] of airspeed, and were making just eighty knots over the ground." Once Rob Kornexl had entered his flight plan into the computer, they headed north up the coast toward Dutch Harbor. "We had a left quartering wind on our tail," adds Eason, "and were were getting jackhammered pretty good, bouncing around, and crabbing [flying cocked sideways] the entire time. But you couldn't tell, because it was darker than a well-digger's ass out there!

"Then our ground speed really began to pick up," Eason continues. "And when we actually turned into Unalaska Bay, towards the end of the airport runway there on the west side of Ballyhoo Mountain, the williwaws were rolling down off the mountain slopes, and swirling around Hog Island, and we were making something like 170 knots [195 mph] of ground speed. That's when we decided that, with all that wind behind us, we really needed to slow it down. We couldn't see Dutch Harbor at all."

Once during a similar winter blow, a cargo plane plowed into a nearby hillside on approach to the primitive airport. Coast Guard search-and-rescue personnel were able to place the frozen, crash-compacted bodies of the two pilots—the only victims in the crash—inside the rescue basket at the same time.

When the H-65 finally landed back in Dutch Harbor, its engines had been shut down, and everyone had safely deboarded, Tim Eason walked over, grabbed Aaron Bean, and hugged him. "Brother, I'm glad you made it," he said. Greg Gibbons and Rob Kornexl made similar gestures.

Aaron Bean and Captain Singh were taken directly to the hospital and treated for hypothermia. With their two survivors gone, Eason and his crew, with the help of several ground-crew members, pushed the H-65 into the Pinn Air hangar on the north side of the field.

Having arrived at the end of their mission, the flight

crew experienced a substantial adrenaline dump. Standing inside the hangar in a well-lit space, they were able to take a closer look at the helicopter that had done it all. The inside of the rear cabin was so coated in oil and jet fuel, it was almost black.

Upon closer inspection they found what are referred to as "witness marks" on the metal underside of the aircraft's tail. These long, black marks revealed where the hoist cable had repeatedly rubbed up against it. The winds had apparently blown the rescue basket so far aft that it sailed virtually horizontal at times. The basket, too, was solid black, completely coated in oil. The red foam floats that were mounted on either end of the basket soon became collector's items for souvenir seekers.

Now, as Tim Eason stood studying the battle scars on the H-65, he began to sense the gravity of the overall experience, and the difficulty of the tasks undertaken. It had been a remarkable mission, and as he continued to "roll off" the intense emotional pitch that he and his men had maintained, Eason found himself standing there beside his helicopter in a kind of stupified silence, wondering silently to himself, "What the hell did we just do?"

He walked over to use the hangar phone, then. He needed to make a quick call to his wife MaryAnn back in Kodiak. She'd probably already heard that a USCG helicopter had crashed during a rescue attempt in the Bering

Sea, and was no doubt worried sick. His call to her was short and to the point.

"Honey, you know I love you," he began. "And you've probably heard what happened. But we're okay. We're back in Dutch now . . ." He closed their private conversation by saying "I have to go, now. I'll give you another call in a little while."

Once their H-65 had been serviced and put to bed, Eason, Kornexl, and Gibbons caught a ride to the Grand Aleutian Hotel to check in. Doug Watson, Dave Neel, Brian Lickfield, and Aaron Bean soon joined them in the Cape Cheerful Bar. It was an emotional reunion.

After their initial greeting and thanks, Eason and his crew went to their rooms, showered, changed clothes, and met back in the lounge again, where they held their own "critical incident stress management debriefing, over some cold, carbonated, adult beverages."

"When we go out on a mission," says Tim Eason, "we sign a blue sheet, essentially checking out our plane. And when we get back from a flight, we close the blue sheet by describing the mission, what time we took off, the time of our return, what happened and when—essentially checking the aircraft back in." It was with that understanding, then, that Eason approached Dave Neel and jokingly asked, "Well, pal, your aircraft is somewhere on the bottom of the Bering Sea. So, what I want to know is, how are you going to close out that blue sheet?"

■   ■   ■

The next day, Tim Eason and his crew were ordered to deliver the H-65 chopper to Cold Bay along a route that completely bypassed the shipwrecked remains of the *Selendang Ayu*. Volatile weather in the form of wind, rain, and snow can continue for months in the Bering Sea—but, ironically, by the next morning the raging seas and darkness were gone, and a cold but dazzling winter's day had replaced them. In spite of its low December orbit, the sun shone down on the vast, shimmering blue waters of the Bering Sea, which lay astonishingly smooth, as far as one could see.

Rob Kornexl would later describe it as "the classic, quintessential, morning-after-the-storm." Tim Eason recalls that during their noon flight back to Cold Bay, "the skies were blue, the wind was calm, and we climbed up high and enjoyed a beautiful Alaskan day."

Upon arrival at the base hangar in Kodiak, the crewmen of the 6020 were greeted by a crowd of people, including reporters and photographers. Fellow Coasties also formed a line in honor of them. And then Neel, Watson, Lickfield, and Bean—some of the select few to have ever lived through a chopper crash—walked the gauntlet, so to speak, shaking the hands of each.

"Congratulations!" said one fellow Coastie. "Good job."
"Glad to see you made it back alive," offered another.
"Way to hang it out there, buddy."

It was an emotional experience for everyone. Brian Lickfield embraced his wife Becky and, picking up the youngest of four sons, hugged them all. He was INDEED glad to be back home once again, with both feet planted on terra firma. The rest of the crew had similar encounters.

Having first delivered their H-65 Dolphin to Cold Bay, Tim Eason, Rob Kornexl, and Greg Gibbons were greeted aboard a C-12 Air Force transport by Admiral Olson. When they arrived in Kodiak several hours later they, too, were welcomed home by their Coast Guard comrades, and by their families as well. A moving photo of Tim Eason, smiling broadly with his wife MaryAnn, and carrying his small daughter Samantha was printed the next day on the front cover of Alaska's only statewide newspaper *The Anchorage Daily News*. The look of joy and relief etched across his face is unmistakable.

EPILOGUE

Short of wartime missions in Iraq, or Special Forces action behind enemy lines in Afghanistan, there was probably not another cadre of helicopter pilots and their crews anywhere in the armed services that year who faced dangers and challenges comparable to those who flew on the *Selendang Ayu* mission in the Bering Sea in December of 2004.

The H-60 flight crew of Dave Neel, Doug Watson, Brian Lickfield, and Aaron Bean, the H-65's crew of Tim Eason, Rob Kornexl, and Greg Gibbons, as well as Doug Cameron and his crew, and Cdr. Matt Bell and his people on the *Alex Haley*, had ventured with daring to the very edge of the precipice, launched into the abyss, and returned from their individual odysseys with vivid tales of the living and the dead.

Dave Neel

As the research for and writing of this book comes to a close, Cdr. Dave Neel and his family are stationed in Sitka, Alaska. He is, once again, carrying out his patrols in that treacherous region from the commander's seat of an H-60 Jayhawk.

Performing death-defying acts of heroism to hoist a crew of terrified mariners off a sinking ship in a wild winter storm at night in Alaska's Bering Sea, is the dream of every true search-and-rescue pilot. Dave Neel knows today that the mission he and his squad launched out on was a noble cause. Saving the lives of nineteen crewmen from certain death, people he did not know and had never met, was the very definition of service above self.

As the years pass and the details of this rescue mission slide further into the annals of history, in his mind's eye Dave Neel still returns to the night of that unexpected calamity. Like any human being caught up in the mind-bending stress of such a horrendous event, certain moments elude him. Recalling his experience for this book, and still pressing for the answers, he asks himself, "What happened, exactly? Did I do something wrong? Should I have done something differently?"

But, I remind him, who could have anticipated the monster wave that came powering out of the night, striking at precisely the wrong moment, or the gigantic fountain of spume that washed his H-60 out of the sky?

Since the wreck, Dave Neel says he has often given thanks to the God above that the crash occurred when it did. Had he and Doug Watson been unable to clear the side of the ship on their way down, the impact on all those aboard their H-60 would have been "catastrophic." Neel is certain that had they "crashed on the deck of the ship and broken up, all of us would have died."

He also offers up a heartfelt thanks to Tim Eason, Rob Kornexl, and Greg Gibbons, as well as Cdr. Matt Bell and his people, and Dale Estilette and his flight crew.

"If the H-65 had been tied down on the back deck of the *Alex Haley* when we crashed," Neel adds, "we wouldn't have had a chance. Even if the 65 had been ordered into the air at the very moment we went into the water, we would not have had a chance. When they picked me up out of the water, I had just minutes left to live, because I was heading into the surf zone. It was waiting for me.

"I'm telling you, there was a lot of providence on that first day, because the very moment that H-65 lifted off of the back deck of the *Alex Haley*, our radio communications [one of the most sophisticated systems on earth] were instantly restored.

"You know, if that helicopter had not taken off right then, I'd be dead," reiterates Neel. "I mean, there is no doubt in my mind. I've seen what a surf zone filled with boulders and volcanic rock and lined with cliffs hundreds of feet high can do to a human being. It strips the clothes off their bodies. I was being carried along at a really fast clip by the currents. There was no swimming out of it. I had nowhere else to go. And those seas were sixty feet high in some cases. I mean, I was a dead man, and I knew it."

Tim Eason

For their courageous and decisive actions in the face of grave danger while saving six lives, Tim Eason, Rob Kornexl, and Greg Gibbons were awarded the Distinguished Flying Cross (DFC), one of the most prestigious medals a military pilot and his crew can receive. They were also singled out by the Naval Helicopter Association as 2005's Air Crew of the Year for their heroic actions that night.

Tim Eason looks back on the incident with mixed feelings. "I am very proud to wear the medal," he says today. "But I'd happily trade my DFC for the lives of those six civilians. Yet it wasn't to be. We go out and do what we do because we want to save lives. That's what Cdr. Neel and his crew were trying to do. This case was tragic because six lives were lost. In the end, we did manage to save twenty civilian lives and four Coasties. But the raw reality of the Bering Sea is that it is a ruthless and unforgiving environment. We don't have to make up stories about how rough it was that night. That storm took a 738-foot-long freighter and broke it in half like a toothpick!

"If those guys had gotten into the basket in a reasonably quick and orderly fashion," adds Eason, "we would have been out of there by the time that big wave hit. But when we put the basket down, nobody got in it. Then we had to put Aaron in the basket and send him down. So that was two extra hoist evolutions. Of course that's 20/20, too. You can what-if the hell out of what happened that night.

"If we had taken off from the *Alex Haley* a few minutes earlier," Eason adds, "those guys wouldn't have been on-scene, and we would have been hoisting and it could have very well been us that crashed. I don't know if a smaller helicopter like ours would have fared as well in such a crash. We may have all perished."

Had they taken even a couple of minutes more to set up the H-65 and launch it, Tim Eason and his men probably wouldn't have been allowed to take off from the *Alex Haley* at all, because with the H-60 already on-scene, it wouldn't have been deemed necessary. "And if we wouldn't have taken off," he adds, "they probably would have died before we could have gotten to them. They would have been beaten to death against the rocks.

"Even though our air crewmen in the water were wearing dry suits with life vests and helmets, had we not been hovering right there on-scene behind those guys, they would have been crushed on the shoreline before we could have lifted off the flight deck of the *Alex Haley*. We had thirty-five-foot breaking seas crashing on the rocky base of those cliffs. I don't think any of them would have survived. So a good part of it certainly was providence, the timing, otherwise, we wouldn't have been there for them, or they wouldn't have been there for us."

The facts also have led Tim Eason to believe that had they been unable to rescue the men during the night, stranded as they were on the bow of the dismembered freighter, Captain Singh would have almost certainly died from hypothermia. Aaron Bean, who was in such remarkable physical condition, may have survived it, but clad as he was in only a dry suit, when they finally pulled him into the aircraft, "he was already very, very cold."

By the time they landed in Dutch Harbor, Eason and his crew had logged just 3.3 hours of total flight time. "But trust me," says Eason. "It seemed like a lot longer than that. I mean, we were working our butts off, all three of us, on every one of those hoists. Rob was backing me up with altitude and obstacles, and whenever he was flying, I was backing him up. It took all three of us to effect those recoveries."

Pat Bacher

As the pilot of the H-60 who, along with Doug Cameron, was forced to return to Cold Bay, Pat Bacher says, "I firmly believe that those six people who died is on that skipper's shoulders."

But there was something more that, in retrospect, still haunts him. He adds, "I remember our flight mech Andy Fumala saying something to the effect of one of the crewmen [about to climb into their rescue basket] on deck has got a big bag of luggage with him. And Doug and I looked at each other and said, 'There's no room for any luggage.'" Doug Cameron ordered Fumala to lower the crewman back down so he could discard his luggage, and set a precedent for the others.

"But when the rescue basket hit the deck," adds Bacher, "he got out of the basket. I guess whatever was in that bag was very valuable to him, because he ran off with it, and then somebody else came and got in. Ultimately, I think he was one of those people who ended up dying in the crash. That's something that still sticks with me. The decision that that guy made ultimately cost him his life."

Rob Kornexl

"For what its worth," notes co-pilot Rob Kornexl, "if you're going to portray a hero in this book, Greg Gibbons is your man. There are not words to describe what an amazing job he did. It was a phenomenal effort on his part, both [in] pulling the guys out of the water initially, and, in particular, managing the cable and basket. I mean, we were flying that helicopter all *over* the sky trying to keep it under control.

"Lord only knows how many times we nearly got that hoist cable and basket tangled up in the ship's rigging," continues Kornexl. "I don't even *want* to know how close it came. Had that happened, it would have meant the end of our hoisting operations, and those men would have very likely died. But somehow Greg kept it clear."

With no other means at his disposal, says Kornexl, Greg Gibbons decided to try to use the rescue basket to literally scoop the man up. "There are no words to describe how difficult this is from two hundred feet in the air on such a night as that."

Watching from down on the bow of the freighter below, Aaron Bean readily agrees. "Greg Gibbons saved my life," he says. "He was amazing. It was really something to see. I mean, it was incredible!"

Aaron Bean

Aaron Bean will be long remembered as the rescue swimmer who took the ship's captain under his care, persevered through countless dangers and difficulties, and ultimately saved the man's life. "The opportunity to help another survive does not come along all that often," Aaron recalled for me, during one of several tape-recorded interviews. "It is not the kind of thing a rescue swimmer gets to do every day. It doesn't come along every time you are on duty.

"Even if he [Captain Singh] was, like, cold and lifeless I wouldn't have abandoned him. I would not have let him go. If I had to go down [trying], I would go down. I would have given my life so that that ship's captain might live. But that is what we do. There is no other choice." He pauses. "I put my hands on all twenty-six men during that SAR case. It was an honor to have done so."

The hard truth, as Bean saw it, was that "the rescue basket was right in front of them. All they would have had to do was stand up and take a few steps forward." By refusing to climb in, they unnecessarily prolonged the time it should have taken to execute the rescue and forced Doug Watson to "hang there in the air" for such an impossibly long time—a fact that ultimately sealed their own fates.

Aaron Bean also believes that had he been in the back of the copter at the time of the crash, strapped into his seat along with Brian Lickfield and the seven recently hoisted sailors, he, too, would have likely perished. For in all the months of incredibly intensive rescue swimmer's training that Bean had gone through, "not once" did he practice escaping from the inverted cabin of a recently crashed helicopter while wearing a gunner's belt. "Never," he says. His fate, he suspects, would have likely been the same as the others in back who drowned and were never seen again.

Bean would ultimately be awarded the Air Medal for his tenacious efforts in saving the life of the freighter's captain on that unforgettable Alaskan night. And many are those who feel that he clearly deserved the DFC. When I last spoke with him he had left the Coast Guard, and he and his wife Jen were attending a major West Coast university where he was finishing up a degree in anthropology. "I don't exercise as much as I used to," he says, "because I spend most of my time carrying my textbooks up the stairs of our library." But he often thinks about that mission in the Bering Sea, and how it all came down.

"It could have worked out so well," he adds, "but for

the timing. We could have saved them all. One rogue wave."

Matt Bell

Summarizing the night, and the roller-coaster ride of emotions that the crew of the *Alex Haley* experienced, Cdr. Matt Bell says, "We were up when the tugboat arrived on-scene, and again when they got our towline strung over to the freighter, and then we were down when the towline broke. Then we were up when they dropped the anchor overboard, and back down again when it parted. We got our helo [H-65] up, and man, we're feeling good! Then the worst accident that can happen, happens. And we're down again.

"Everybody asks me how big those waves were out there. And I say, 'Well, I can't tell you officially how big they were.' But I can remember sitting in my chair [thirty-six feet above the flat waterline] and having to lean over and look *up* out the upper half of my front windows to see the tops of some of those waves as they passed! If we had been on any other of our cutters [due to the severity of the storm, and the somewhat unstable trim characteristics of the longer, newer, narrower, and more expensive models], our H-65 wouldn't have been able to lift off."

"Thank God we got the helicopter into the air. Otherwise there'd be all these people in the water with no one on hand to save them. If Dave Neel's 60 had shown up at any time earlier, I would not have launched the 65. If our timing had been off, and we'd waited for even another five minutes, the 60 would have been on-scene, and our 65 would not have been in the air. The only reason those people are alive is because our H-65 was hovering over them, watching them . . . at the time of the crash. It was by divine intervention that they were there when they needed to be."

As for the six crewmen who died in the crash: "It's the worst feeling, because there's not a thing you can do about it. The first eighteen people we took off didn't perish. I feel really bad for the folks, and the families of those who lost their lives. But I can look back at it and say 'Hey, there are nineteen who did come back alive!'

"As for the captain of the *Selendang Ayu*, hindsight is 20/20. Sorry, but I'm not going to be the guy out there who judges him. We're going to be as professional as we can about it. Of course we had frustrations. We're out there to prevent hazards, to prevent casualties at sea. We did our best to offer our assistance, and to try and get those crewmen off. But in the end, he is the master of the vessel.

"Do I think that he waited too long to get his crew off? Absolutely. But here I have a master who's responsible for his ship, responsible for his men, responsible for his cargo, responsible back to the company who owns the ship."

As for Aaron Bean, "He was just a kid," adds Cdr. Matt Bell, now Captain Matt Bell, speaking to me from his office as commodore of the USCG's Persian Gulf Fleet in Bahrain. "But for a young man like him to stand on the deck of that ship and remain as cool, calm, and collected as he did, in the midst of the ship breaking up all around him, that was pretty impressive. I think the term *hero* gets overblown a lot, but Aaron Bean's actions that night were downright heroic. Just amazing!"

Brian Lickfield

In 2007, having completed twenty years in the Coast Guard, Brian Lickfield retired. In reference to how life and death was meted out during that mission in the Bering Sea, he says, "I think about it every day. It's probably going to affect me the rest of my life." Pressed for more specifics regarding Captain Singh, the night of the crash, and his feelings about how it all went down, Brian says, "It was just so frustrating. It should have been a done deal, but no one took charge. They wouldn't get off the boat."

Lickfield knows now, however, that while he and his crewmates were not able to save everyone, they did make a difference. During that mission, they managed to save the lives of no less than twenty of the twenty-six sailors that the SAR teams had set out to rescue. Since then, he's come to accept that there was absolutely nothing more anyone could have done. He was just lucky to have survived.

While the experience was traumatic, Lickfield likes to quote Brad Pitt in the movie *Fight Club:* "Only after a disaster can we be resurrected."

Since his retirement, Brian Lickfield found a job in Kodiak, hauling unlimited freight loads on flatbed tractor trailer rigs. He enjoys the work. "Sometimes I feel like I should be paying *them*," he says. "But the thing I like best about my job is not having to worry about going swimming unexpectedly."

At home each night with his wife Rebecca and his four boys, he has come to love the life they have put together. In short, they're dug in. Brian was originally from upstate New York. His wife Becky, Massachusetts. But they soon discovered that the extreme weather in Kodiak is quite similar to the "snow belt" winters they knew back home. In addition, the education system in the area is exceptional. As for sports, a child only has to choose. "Becky is a soccer mom," Brian adds. "She carts everyone around to their games."

Like most people who make their home in Alaska, they've especially come to embrace the long summer days when school is out and the kids are free to run, hike, fish, and go four-wheeling. "Our kids have definitely seen and experienced things they never would down south," Brian adds. "The boys and I love to fish. And silver salmon run like crazy here. We know a couple of nice fishing holes out on the Buskin [River]."

He recalls that once, when they were fishing there, a huge Kodiak brown bear wandered out onto the opposite river bank directly across from them, just thirty yards away. "He was pretty impressive," says Lickfield. "He stood up and began scratching his back on a tree." Then he waded out into the river to try and intercept a passing fish. Biting into the back of one struggling salmon, he carried it up on the bank and gobbled it completely. Then, obviously unimpressed by the puny human creatures nearby, he laid down and took a nap.

"Another time, we were in our small boat fishing in calm waters off Sitka [in Southeastern Alaska], when a pod of orca's [killer whales] began swimming around us. My wife and boys were there to see it, too. It was awesome! Like something out of *National Geographic*."

Doug Watson

"Looking back, I'm sure we all shared a lot of guilt, the survivor's guilt type of thing," recalls Lcdr. Doug Watson, speaking from his latest assignment in Cape Cod,

Massachusetts. "Nobody has been harder on us than ourselves . . . It took me a while to get back to where I could actually be a useful aircraft commander again. I started to fly H-60s again in January, right after the holiday break. I was doing great. All summer I was flying . . ."

Then in September of 2005, Watson flew an H-60 into a harrowing nighttime rescue mission one hundred miles off Cape Hinchenbrook on the outermost reaches of Alaska's Prince William Sound, in which he was forced to abort a hoist from a sailboat when his rescue swimmer, harnessed and dangling on the end of the hoist cable, went "skipping across the water." It was the strange, disorienting effect of the greasy-smooth groundswells, some as wide as the horizon, rolling past below that got to him.

"Anyway," Watson recalls, "that kind of set me back, kind of retriggered some anxieties that I had. And I came back from the flight thinking, 'You know what, I'm done with this.' "

After landing back in Cordova, Watson called Kodiak and talked with a fellow pilot. " 'You know, I think I'm done,' I told him. 'Stick a fork in me. I think that's it for me.' It wasn't fear. It was more anxiety. But I should have never said 'I'm done,' because I didn't really mean that . . . The only anxiety I had back in Kodiak was hoisting at night over open water. I could fly all day in float planes, and airplanes, and helicopters. And did. I just meant that I needed some time off.

"So I took about a month off from flying, and then I started to get back into it again. I started becoming comfortable in the aircraft. And just about that time, the head of Coast Guard aviation back in D.C. found out that I was apparently having some problems, and he told my C.O. to ground me. . . . So I spent the last two or three months not flying."

Lcdr. Watson ended up in Washington, D.C., on a staff tour for several years, during which time he got "cooled down," he says. "Time heals all wounds. I went through a rough patch." Then, toward the end of his tour in the nation's capital, he began the ultracompetitive application process to qualify for flying fixed-wing aircraft, and was eventually granted a position as the pilot of his first love, the twin-engined jet, the H-25 Falcon.

"I'm real happy to be getting back into the cockpit. I loved the H-60 Jayhawk. I loved flying that helicopter. I would have gladly gone back to them. But I just couldn't pass up the opportunity to go fly an airplane like the Falcon.

"Looking back, if I had to do it all over again, I doubt that I'd do anything differently. You hear about fishing boats sinking in the Bering Sea, and small vessels having trouble all the time. But you'd never anticipate that a freighter that big could be so vulnerable and create such destruction. It doesn't seem possible. That still amazes me to this day."

As for the captain of the *Selendang Ayu,* he adds, "I don't fault the skipper. He was doing what he thought was best at the time. I know he was under a lot of pressure. I can't say that I harbor a resentment for anybody about the way the case was run. It is what it is."

Many of those who were involved directly in the mission and ensuing investigation, however, would place responsibility for the deaths squarely on the master's head, for not getting his men off the ship when he had the chance.

Regardless of fault, a $16 million helicopter was destroyed, a $12 million freighter and its cargo were lost, and six crewmen were killed. Though small, when compared to the eleven-million-gallon Exxon *Valdez* oil spill in Prince William Sound in 1989 that impacted several thousand miles of wilderness coast, the main bulk of the roughly 325,000 gallons of fuel oils that eventually washed ashore Unalaska Island, contaminated the flora and fauna along some twenty-five miles of her pristine shores, and killed hundreds of sea birds and a colony of sea otters. In the long term, the oil contaminants will affect local salmon streams, and sea life such as halibut and codfish.

In the spring of 2006, some fifteen months later, and just as the massive, and largely successful oil cleanup and ship-salvage efforts were coming to an end, Captain Kailash Bhushan Singh pleaded guilty in the Federal Courthouse in Anchorage, Alaska, to the criminal act of lying to investigators. Singh had apparently claimed in his log books that only thirteen hours had passed between the time one of his engineers had mistakenly shut down the freighter's main engine, and his notifying authorities about the problem, when, in fact, a total of fifteen hours had elapsed.

In retrospect, it was not exactly an earth-shattering indiscretion. And one that could easily be attributed to the extreme stress and the largely sleepless, mind-numbing vigil the captain was said to have kept virtually throughout the duration of the intensely unpredictable two-and-a-half day drama that he presided over.

In truth, no maritime law exists on the books today that would prevent the captain of a freighter underway on the high seas anywhere in the world from doing exactly as he pleases. A captain's rule aboard such vessels remains absolute. Inviolable. Captain Singh's decisions pertaining to the release of individual members of his crew, in regards to who went where and when, were his to make at his own discretion throughout the entire episode.

Singh's legal counselor, Mr. Michael Chalos, probably the finest maritime attorney in all of America—he also successfully defended Joe Hazelwood, the captain of the Exxon *Valdez*—rightly argued in court that in such brutal weather, the two hours in question would have made absolutely no difference in the final outcome of the drama that played out in the Bering Sea that December. It would not have prevented the grounding of the *Selendang Ayu,* nor the breakup and oil spill that followed.

The court, at least by severity of punishment, seemed to agree. Captain Singh received just three years of probation and a one-hundred-dollar fine. Refusing to speak with the press, Singh flew home to India. Repeated attempts by this author to interview him also proved unsuccessful.

And so I must take my leave of this multifaceted adventure. My efforts to chronicle it, over the course of several years, now, have finally come to an end. Others have written about the biological impact of the spill, the mopping up efforts, the fines levied, and the $98 million the MCI shipping group that owned the *Selendang Ayu* ultimately had to pay.

But I would be remiss if I failed to mention the many acts of kindness and generosity the people of Unalaska and Dutch Harbor bestowed upon the shipwrecked sailors who found themselves stranded in that frozen, windswept reach of the Aleutian Islands. Far from their homes back in India and the Philippines, many of these shivering survivors had lost their shoes to the ship's violent deck wash. Most had been forced to leave their luggage behind as well.

Organizing quickly, and spreading Christmas cheer as they went, area residents came together and provided them with footware and dry clothing, hot food and drink, and fellowship. Cooking facilities were furnished by the folks at The Grand Aleutian Hotel. All in all, it was a spontaneous outpouring of warm-hearted hospitality, one for the history books, and bona fide proof that Alaska's indomitable spirit lives on.

ACKNOWLEDGMENTS

Most emphatically, I now wish to note those Coast Guardsmen who were directly involved in this epic rescue mission.

The crew of the H-60 helicopter #6020: Lt. Doug Watson, pilot from Cranford, New Jersey; Lt. Dave Neel, co-pilot and commander of the aircraft, from Stilwell, Oklahoma; Petty Officer Brian Lickfield, the flight mechanic from Allentown, Pennsylvania; and Petty Officer Third Class Aaron Bean, that amazing young rescue swimmer from Silvertown, Colorado.

The crew of the H-60 helicopter #6021, including: Lt. Doug Cameron from Astoria, Oregon; Lt. Pat Becher of

Mobile, Alabama; AMT3 Andy Famula, the flight mechanic from San Diego, California; and AST3 Joey "the Grizz" Gryzenia.

The crew of the USCG cutter *Alex Haley,* including: Capt. Matt Bell of Kodiak, Alaska; Senior Chief Dale Estilette, the cutter's flight deck crew boss from Morgan City, Louisiana; Petty Officer Steven Schmid; and the ninety-six other crew members, both male and female, on that same cutter; and the crow's nest lookout on watch that night whom I could never locate.

The crew of the H-65 helicopter #6065, also on board the CG cutter *Alex Haley,* including: Lt. Tim Eason, the pilot from Savannah, Georgia; Rob Kornexl, the co-pilot from upstate Michigan; and flight mechanic Greg Gibbons.

I also received assistance, in one form or another, from Capt. Bill Deal, Commanding Officer of USCG Air Station Kodiak; CDR Russ Zullick (Ret.); CDR John Whiddon (Ret.); Capt. Bill Wade (Ret.); CDR Malcolm Smith (Ret.); Dr. Martin J. Nimerof (Ret.); Lt. Brian McLoughlin; Rescue Swimmers Wil Milum (Ret.), Joe Ungerheier, and Joe Metzler; and those two humble, self-effacing stars of Kevin Costner's action movie *The Guardian,* rescue swimmer Joseph "Butch" Flythe, and that H-60 pilot extraordinaire, CDR Dan Molthen.

Back to the realm of the merely mortal, I must thank my good friend Carl Waldow, the owner of the Cascade Mountain property upon which I both lived and worked over a span of several years. His kindness and generosity throughout the writing of the book shall not be forgotten.

Many thanks must also go out to Cheryl Miller for putting her modern computer to work for me whenever my ancient 1980s-era Apple 2-E word processor reached the finite end of its capabilities. And ever and always, my deepest gratitude goes out to Mrs. Velda Sutton, to my sweethearts Clara Lincoln and Becky Bafford, to my pal Dan Evans, and to friends Larry and Bonnie Keith. I am also indebted to Mrs. Cathy Carlile and Mrs. Janice James, my human spell-checkers, for proofreading the first chaotic draft of the manuscript; and, later, Mrs. Deborah Steele Hazen, owner of *The Clatskanie Chief,* one of the finest small-town newspapers in the West, for offering her editorial insights as well.

Finally, I need to thank my talented and fearless literary agent and attorney in the world of arts and entertainment, Mr. Lance Rosen. He is a rock. Expressed appreciation must also go out to Mr. Marc Resnick, my executive editor at St. Martin's Press, and Ms. Sarah Lumnah, assistant editor. Their learned assistance over the course of this project proved indespensable.

In addition, I would like to thank the following people for their help and encouragement: Jim Gray, owner of Team Electronics in Longview, Washington; Wayne and Sue Sutton; Stan and Cindy Sawyer; Jack Kelly and his wife Donnie; Bob Carlile; David Waldow; Sib Cryblskey;

Aaron "Ace" McClellan; Aaron Whiting; Leroy "Jogger Logger" James; Rick Malinowski; and my spiritual confidant and guru, ninety-three-year-old Joe Garcia.

Special thanks also go to Rob Doer, Gary and Diane Fountain, Steve and Karen Gray, Jerry Marston, the late Steve Johnson, Colleen Geilenfeldt, Todd and Sarah Lippold, Duane and Diane Fredrickson, Jimmy and Martha Turner, Jay and Jean Shaw, Arnie and Carol Turner, the indomitable Mark Baldwin, Pam and Eric Sellix, Rob Walker, Ron "wild man" Williams, Wendi Mudge, Bruce Jolma, and that salty old sea-dog Jon Norgaard. In addition, thanks also to my 6 A.M. wakeup crowd at Nick's Bar and Grill: Idy Gilbert, Frank Molten, and Charlie Campbell, philosophers one and all!

Also, with a heart as large as a pumpkin, thanks to Big Dave Nudo, the late Ethel "mom" Bangert, Chris "Bear Man" Miller, Mark Nelson, Paul "take down" Redburn, Don "smoke jumper" Redburn, Bert and Roseanne Scott, John and Cathy Ludahl, George and Cecile Watson, Leslie Strong, Steven Walker, Warren and Diana Schiehle, Don and Ann Grone, Big Jim Furnish, Pat O'Malley, Pat Levis, Hal Pinkcombe, and Buzz and Bill Roach. In southeast Alaska, thanks to my hot-blooded gal pal Debbie Schiedler, and former logging camp buddy Roger Stidolph and his lovely wife Betty.

Last but not least, in Unalaska, I must acknowledge Mayor Shirley Marquardt; City Manager Chris Hladick;

John and Sue Honen; David Magone; and the salvage king himself, Dan Magone, and his wife, Sue.

If any of the participants, or anyone else, would like to share additional information about the events portrayed in this book please feel free to e-mail me through my contact person at spike.walker@yahoo.com.